ARRESTING HOPE

Women Taking Action in Prison Health Inside Out

edited by

**RUTH ELWOOD MARTIN, MO KORCHINSKI,
LYNN FELS AND CARL LEGGO**

INANNA Publications and Education Inc.
Toronto, Canada

ARRESTING HOPE

Published in Canada by
Inanna Publications and Education Inc.
210 Founders College, York University
4700 Keele Street, Toronto, Ontario M3J 1P3
Telephone: (416) 736-5356 Fax (416) 736-5765
Email: inanna.publications@inanna.ca Website: www.inanna.ca

The publisher gratefully acknowledges the support of the Canada Council for the Arts and the Ontario Arts Council for its publishing program. We also acknowlege the financial assistance of the Government of Canada through the Canada Book Fund,

Note from the publisher: Care has been taken to trace the ownership of copyright material used in this book. The authors and the publisher welcome any information enabling them to rectify any references or credits in subsequent editions.

Cover artwork: Mo Korchinski
Cover design: Val Fullard

Library and Archives Canada Cataloguing in Publication

      Arresting hope : women taking action in prison health inside out /
Ruth Elwood Martin, Mo Korchinski, Lynn Fels & Carl Leggo, editors.

Issued in print and electronic formats.
ISBN 978-1-77133-158-6 (pbk.).— ISBN 978-1-77133-161-6 (pdf).—
ISBN 978-1-77133-159-3 (epub)

      1. Alouette Correctional Centre for Women—Biography. 2. Hope.
I. Martin, Ruth Elwood, 1954–, editor II. Korchinski, Mo, 1966–, editor
III. Fels, Lynn, 1955–, editor IV. Leggo, Carl, 1953–, editor V. Title.

HV9509.B72A58 2014   365'.4309711   C2014-905743-1
                                          C2014-905744-X

MIX
Paper from
responsible sources
FSC
www.fsc.org FSC® C004071

Printed and Bound in Canada.

For all the women still stuck in the revolving door,
the women who have passed away, and the
women who continue to fight the demons of addiction
or bear the burden of trauma and loss.
For the women who have "unlocked the gate"
and are living lives filled with
hope, possibility, and accomplishment.

Table of Contents

Acknowledgements

This book would not have been written without the support and dedication of a great many people. We heartily thank the expansive community of people who contributed to this work.

Firstly, we acknowledge the women whose words within these pages speak to their experiences, and all the women who were in this prison between 2004–2007.

Secondly, we acknowledge all those who have worked towards a new understanding of community behind the gates: recognizing women, their stories, and the hope that refused to be arrested. To warden Brenda Tole for creating the vision, and to the deputy wardens who supported her vision; to Alison Granger-Brown for her courage and energy and commitment to time and hope; to Lara-Lisa Condello, to Linnea Groom and the W2 workers (and their "rent a friend" program); to Aboriginal Elder Holy Cow (Mary Fayant), prison Chaplain Henk Smidstra, and to the guards, contractors, staff, and community agency volunteers who brought their talents, expertise, compassion, and commitment through the gates. In addition, representatives of numerous community organizations attended the prison participatory research forums as guests (see complete list at www.womenin2healing. org/research-projects). Their presence and support provided invaluable affirmation for the women's research work.

Thirdly, we acknowledge the organizations that have funded this work. The Vancouver Foundation supported and believed in this project over the years, and provided an operating grant from the British Columbia Medical Services Fund (BCMSF) entitled "Community-based Participatory Action Research: Collaborating with Women in Prison to

Improve Their Health" (2007); an operating grant entitled, "Community-based Participatory Action Research: Women in2 Healing, Women Who Were Incarcerated" (2008); a BCMSF salary award for Dr. Ruth Elwood Martin entitled, "Community-based Clinical Investigator" with the University of British Columbia Department of Family Practice (2007–2012); and a BCMSF community engagement grant for "Book Proposal, 'Prisons that Heal'" (2010). In addition, the Fraser Health Authority and the Tula Foundation supported this project with operating funds entitled "Participatory Action Research: Women in2 Healing, Women Who Were Incarcerated" (2008). We also acknowledge the many other organizations and individuals who donated funds to the participatory research activities of Women in2 Healing so that incarcerated women can take educational courses, present their work at conferences, host networking events for women with previous incarceration experience, and support venues for women who exit from prison. A complete list of publications and presentations arising from the participatory research project is available on-line at "What We've Done" (www.womenin2healing.org/whatdone).

Fourthly, we thank the Nicola Valley Institute of Technology (NVIT) for their support. In particular, we acknowledge NVIT for hosting monthly support meetings of Women in2 Healing and the writing workshops that spurred the writings in this book. In addition, we are indebted to the University of British Columbia Department of Family Practice and the Women's Health Research Institute, BC Women's Hospital, and the Provincial Health Services Authority for providing practical support such as office space, fiscal hosting, and human resources and administrative support.

Finally, we acknowledge the assistance of Daniel Martin, Gerda Wever, Rebecca James, Lindi Lewis, and Stanley Martin in formatting, editing, designing, and proofreading the various versions of the manuscript and bibliography. Ruth's book group members provided invaluable support with their affirmations following their reading of the first draft. And, we thank Luciana Ricciutelli, Editor-in-Chief of Inanna Publications, for her faith in the manuscript, her expertise, and her thoughtful oversight of the publication of *Arresting Hope*.

Preface

THIS BOOK IS NOT THE RESULT of a solitary prison doctor seeking to improve prison health for women. Rather, this book is born out of a participatory and collaborative process bearing witness to health and healing inside the Alouette Correctional Centre for Women (ACCW).

Women's lives were transformed as a result of participatory processes adopted by the prison warden and prison managers who sought to create a therapeutic environment. As incarcerated women were offered, and assumed, increasing responsibility for all aspects of their lives, so they developed skills and capacities, and they became mentally, physically, and socially healthier. The narratives in this book illuminate a prison community seeking and attaining well-being and highlight the elements of a successful prison.

Between 2005 and 2007, women inside the gates recorded their voices and stories as part of a unique prison participatory health research project led by Ruth Elwood Martin. She engaged incarcerated women as research team members in partnership with university researchers in exploring one overarching question, "How can we improve the health of women in prison?" What began as a health initiative became an educational and cross-disciplinary venture in collaborative learning, care, and community.

It takes tremendous courage for women to go back in time, to dig into their memory, to re-live traumatic formative years, and to write. They travel back to remember, because they want to make sense of their present; they want to understand, so they can heal and move forward; they want to contribute to the learning of others. Lynn Fels and Carl Leggo, academic co-investigators in the prison research project, edited and shaped the writing that we received as the book project began to unfold. Mo Korchinski took a leadership role in the project. Mo edited the evolving manuscript and contributed reflections, poetry, and narratives. She also facilitated a Women in2 Healing meeting to compile women's stories. In addition, Mo created all of the book's illustrations, using lead pencil and charcoal on paper.

We signed a Research Agreement with the BC Corrections Branch of the BC Ministry of Solicitor General to enable us to conduct participatory health research inside Alouette Correctional Centre for Women. The University of British Columbia Behavioural Research Ethics Board provided their certificate of approval for this project.

Net proceeds from the sale of *Arresting Hope* will be used to provide educational bursaries for women with incarceration experience and/ or their families, through donations to the Collaborating Centre for Prison Health and Education (CCPHE) (www.ccphe.ubc.ca) or Womenin2Healing (Win2H) (www.womenin2healing.org).

Arresting Hope

MO KORCHINKSI

Cold steel shimmering chains
Rattling time from the deep dark chimes
Arrested again high on crime
Sentenced to do some long hard time
Off to jail, how hard is this
Waste of time, waste a high
Drumming the drum
Singing the songs

Love me till I can find myself
Found a new life right in front of my eyes
Healing the wounds that left scars that will last
Never forget, but forgive those monsters in the shadows of time
Learn to have hope to cope without dope
Arresting hope to unlock the key
Finding your voice from paragraphs of passion
Listen to the whispers the wild wind blows
Breaking the chains from years of abuse
Time to heal, the past is the past

An Invitation to Readers

THIS BOOK TELLS A STORY about women in a provincial prison in Canada, about how creative leadership fostered opportunities for transformation and hope, and about how engaging in research and writing contributed to healing. The book involves many people, but it is focused on five remarkable women: a doctor, a warden, a recreation therapist, an educator, and an inmate. Christina Baldwin claimed that "story heals" (42). As a collective of four co-editors, we all share the conviction that we need to tell more stories. We agree with Baldwin that "when we live in a family, a community, a country where we know each other's true stories, we remember our capacity to lean in and love each other into wholeness" (18). In order to learn to live together in the ways of connection, hope, and generosity, we must narrate our lives, and we must hear the stories of others. Together, we break silences, tell the truths of our lives, and learn how to listen to the stories of others as a commitment to living with healing and wellness.

While stories are personal, individual, and subjective, the personal is also universal. Our personal stories are connected to history. We are all inextricably and integrally connected as human beings. So, when we tell our stories to others, and when we listen to others tell us their stories, we discover that we are all searching for belonging, for home, for community. Parker Palmer claimed that while our culture "separates inner from outer, private from public, personal from professional" (47), "we all live on the Möbius strip" where "there is no 'inside' and 'outside'" (47). According to Palmer, "we are continually engaged in the evolution of self and world—and we have the power to choose, moment by moment, between that which gives life and that which deals death" (48).

Arresting Hope is a unique book for many reasons, but especially because of the way in which the story of the prison is narrated. In social science research, narrative inquiry typically involves three principal dynamics: story, interpretation, and discourse. *Story* is *what happened.* Therefore, story can be researched by asking the journalist's questions: who? what? when? where? why? how? *Interpretation* addresses the basic question of *so what?* In other words, what is the significance of the story? In much social science research, the question of interpretation is often cast as the most important question because so much social science research is about conclusions and implications. The social scientist always asks: *What does all this mean for practice and policy?* But instead of emphasizing story or interpretation, we emphasize the third dynamic of narrative inquiry. *Discourse* is about *how* we tell the story. Discourse refers to the rhetoric of storytelling, the art and science of shaping and constructing a story for communicating to others (Leggo; Chatman).

The purpose of telling our stories is to tell them in ways that open up new possibilities for understanding, wisdom, and transformation. So, our stories need to be told in ways that arrest attention, that call out, that startle, so that we attend to our stories and the stories of others with renewed focus. It is not enough to just tell our stories. We need to learn to tell them in creative ways. This is the heart of story-making and narrative inquiry.

Arresting Hope includes poetry, stories, letters, interviews, fragments of conversations, reflections, memories, quotations, journal entries, creative nonfiction, and scholarly research. Telling the whole story of the Alouette Correctional Centre for Women is an impossibility, simply because there are so many stories lived by so many people. Out of the multiple and diverse possibilities, we are narrating the stories of a group of women who gathered to teach one another, and to share their stories of grief, desire, and hope.

Arresting Hope narrates a complex story with many lines of connection, and it narrates this complex story in a diverse range of texts like fragments of an immense story. Jean Baudrillard noted that "fragmentary writing is, ultimately, democratic writing. Each fragment enjoys an equal distinction" (8). But we also contend that fragmentary writing invites dialogue and imaginative engagement by readers. Instead of attempting to tell the whole story or even a seamless story with a clear and coherent chronology, we invite readers to linger with the fragments, to attend to the composition of the fragments as artistic renderings that evoke and provoke. *Arresting Hope* does not present a linear and straightforward narrative. Instead, it narrates the tangled chaos of lived experience by presenting a complex network of images and stories that evoke an understanding of people and their hopes and desires. By attending to the story as "an archipelago of fragments" (Paz 26), we grow more and more interested in what is not said, the pauses and spaces and gaps, the traces and echoes, the detours and diversions.

Richard Miller declared: "This is my story. But it is not my story only" (176). *Arresting Hope* is an exemplar of transdisciplinary research. Patricia Leavy noted that transdisciplinarity provides a significant way for researchers "to seriously engage with the major issues and problems of our time" by pooling "our resources in the service of addressing complex contemporary problems" (8). Leavy defined transdisciplinarity as "an approach to conducting social research that involves synergistic collaboration between two or more disciplines with high levels of integration between the disciplinary sets of knowledge" (9). *Arresting Hope* involves many people who work across disciplinary boundaries, and who are learning from and listening to one another.

Walter Brueggemann claimed that "human transformative activity depends upon a transformed imagination" (xx). And imagination is integrally connected to language and recognizing "how singularly words, speech, language, and phrase shape consciousness and define reality" (64). Transformation, both personal and political, individual and cultural, depends on remembering and hoping. We need to grieve with compassion and empathy, question with critical energy, and examine creative possibilities with passion and hope. Brueggemann wrote, "the evocation of an alternative reality" involves the creation of "a new rhetoric" (18). Brueggemann called for more poetry, more stories, more imagination:

> The prophet engages in futuring fantasy. The prophet does not ask if the vision can be implemented, for questions of implementation are of no consequence until the vision can be imagined. The *imagination* must come before the *implementation*. (40)

Arresting Hope is a testimony to what is possible when a community of people engage together in imagining alternative possibilities.

As Brueggemann recognized, "speech about hope cannot be explanatory and scientifically argumentative; rather, it must be lyrical in the sense that it touches the hopeless person at many different points" (65). In *Arresting Hope,* we present many voices and write in hopeful ways in order to sustain hearts with abiding hope. We agree with Gregory Orr who testified convincingly to "the survival function of story-making: it helps us to live" (21).

Like Miller, we pursue writing that fosters "a kind of critical optimism that is able to transform idle feelings of hope into viable plans for sustainable action" (27). Miller argued for the value of writing that extends beyond the boundaries of traditional academic discourse, and called for "writing as a place where the personal and the academic, the private and the public, the individual and the institutional, are always inextricably interwoven" (31). Miller invited us to write in diverse ways so each of us can "locate one's evolving narrative within a specific range of institutional contexts, shifting attention from the self to the nexus where the self and institution meet" (138). This is the goal of the kind of life writing that shapes *Arresting Hope*. By writing about the past, we make sense of the past while also generating "a sense of possibility, a sense that a better, brighter future is out there to be secured" (Miller 20).

Arresting Hope reminds us that prisons are not only places of punishment, marginalization, and trauma, but that they can also be places of hope, blessing even, where people with difficult lived experiences can begin to compose stories full of healing, anticipation, communication, education, connection, and community. We are not presenting a romantic or nostalgic version of the story of the Alouette Correctional Centre for Women. We are presenting a story that acknowledges pressing challenges, but we are also eager to present a testimony to how hopefulness is possible in prison. We promote hope because we have been arrested by hope's possibilities.

Arresting Hope is artistic, academic, and activist. With characteristic wisdom, Jean Vanier asked:

> Is this not the life undertaking of us all ... to become human? It can be a long and sometimes painful process. It involves a growth to freedom, an opening up of our hearts to others, no longer hiding behind masks or behind the walls of fear and prejudice. It means discovering our common humanity. (1)

May we always be able to learn from and lean on one another.

REFERENCES

Baldwin, Christina. *Storycatcher: Making Sense of Our Lives through the Power and Practice of Story*. Novato: New World Library, 2005.

Baudrillard, Jean. *Fragments: Cool Memories III, 1991-1995.* Trans. Emily Agar. London: Verso, 1997.

Brueggemann, Walter. *The Prophetic Imagination.* 2nd ed. Minneapolis: Fortress Press, 2001.

Chatman, S. *Story and Discourse: Narrative Structure in Fiction and Film.* Ithaca: Cornell University Press, 1978.

Leavy, Patricia. *Essentials of Transdisciplinary Research: Using Problem-Centered Methodologies.* Walnut Creek, CA: Left Coast Press, 2011.

Leggo, Carl. "Narrative Inquiry: Attending to the Art of Discourse." *Language & Literacy* 10 (1) (2008): 1-21.

Miller, Richard E. *Writing at the End of the World.* Pittsburgh: University of Pittsburgh Press, 2005.

Orr, Gregory. *Poetry as Survival.* Athens: University of Georgia Press, 2002.

Palmer, Parker J. *A Hidden Wholeness: The Journey Toward an Undivided Life.* San Francisco: Jossey-Bass, 2004.

Paz, Octavio. *The Other Voice: Essays on Modern Poetry.* Trans. Helen Lane. New York: Harcourt Brace Jovanovich, 1990.

Vanier, Jean. *Becoming Human.* Toronto: House of Anansi Press, 1998.

Before Prison

In the prison clinic, women tell me about traumatic events they endured as children, young teenagers and women. I put down my pen and listen, bearing witness to their lives. If I had been dealt the same cards, I might have been sitting in their chairs.
—Ruth Elwood Martin, Prison Doctor

Addiction runs strong through my veins.
Escape? There is no escape.

—Melissa Glover

I wanted to be able to close my eyes and feel home, not like I was falling.

—Jen Flavel

Paragraphs of Passion[1]

A

Well, I'd like to do research on recovery and relapse.

B

I want to know why I keep repeating the same mistakes. I want to know how to get out of the entrenched lifestyle I got caught up in. My passion is to learn about manic depression and bi-polar disease.

C

My passion is Crystal Meth. I want to learn what my drug of choice does to my health and how it affects my life.

D

I would like to learn more about mental illness and addiction—to learn what I put in my body and how I can change.

E

I am researching Fetal Alcohol Syndrome and its relationship to crime and drugs. I'd also like to teach others about this disease and its effects.

---

[1]"Paragraphs of Passion" were written by the women who participated as researchers in the participatory health research team in response to the question, "What is your passion?" Writing these paragraphs of passion became the first step in each woman's choice of a research topic. The women then presented power-point presentations about their research topic at community health forums that they hosted inside the correctional centre. In order to protect the women's privacy, we used an alphabetical designation.

Doctor's Journey

RUTH ELWOOD MARTIN

TODAY WAS MY FIRST DAY working in the medical clinic of a women's prison. I felt like I was visiting another planet, passing through those gates, experiencing another world, and learning from people inside it. When a friend told me about this job I thought, "There is no way I can work in a prison clinic; it must the lowest kind of medical job, only for those doctors who can't find any other type of work." Yet, today, I saw more pathology and more tragic medical diagnoses than I see in a year in my regular family practice on the west side of the city. This day has changed my life forever—my view of medical practice will never be the same.

—Journal entry

For sixteen years, I worked as a family physician in the prison medical clinic of a Canadian provincial correctional centre, one or two days a week—sometimes in a male centre, but mostly in the women's correctional centre.

Family physicians do more than treat people when they are ill; they are "the objective witness of their lives" (Berger 109), and they "bear witness" to suffering (Charon 1265). They record patients' health and healing, illness and disease. They listen to patients' life stories; they observe time passing in their faces and their bodies; they rejoice in the resilience of their emotions and spirit, their families, and their communities.

I have witnessed more women with ill health in prison than I ever saw in community practice on the west side of Vancouver. I have provided medical care for incarcerated women with HIV, hepatitis C, endocarditis, and cancer. I have listened to stories of abuse and poverty, hopelessness and substance abuse, depression, anxiety, psychosis, and loneliness. I met women who described a depth of despair that I could only begin

14

to imagine. I also listened to women's stories of resilience and tenacity, their yearnings for improvement and their 'if only' hopes.

Studies show that women entering prisons worldwide suffer more from disease than the general population, including HIV, hepatitis C, endocarditis, skin infections, sexually transmitted diseases, and pre-cancerous cervical lesions (Van Den Bergh, Gatherer, and Møller 406). Women entering prison are also more likely to suffer mental illness, post traumatic stress disorder, and alcohol and drug dependence (Buchanan et al. 96). Underlying these factors is trauma (Van Den Bergh, Gatherer, Fraser, and Møller 690). Incarcerated women also tend to live in poverty and have unstable housing, or are homeless (Richie 368). Women with short prison sentences in Canada (under two years) are usually incarcerated because of a crime related to alcohol and/or substance use (Martin, Gold, Murphy, Remple, Berkovitz, and Money 98, 100).

The greater the number of adverse childhood events that children and young teenagers endure, the more likely they are to encounter the justice system, suffer ill health, and have alcohol and substance use issues over the course of their lifetime (Levin and Becker 54). Adverse childhood events associated with criminality and ill health are traumatic events, particularly abuse and neglect (Levin and Becker 54). In this chapter you will read stories about children and young women, about their lives before their incarceration began.

REFERENCES

Berger, J. *A Fortunate Man: The Story of a Country Doctor.* New York: Vintage Books, 1997.

Charon, R. "What To Do With Stories." *Canadian Family Physician* 53 (8) (2007): 1265-1267

Buchanan, M., K. Murphy, M. S. Martin, M. Korchinski, J. Buxton, A. Granger-Brown, D. Hanson, T. G. Hislop, A. C. Macaulay, and R. E. Martin. "Understanding Incarcerated Women's Perspectives on Substance Use: Catalysts, Reasons for Use, Consequences, and Desire for Change." *Journal of Offender Rehabilitation* 50 (2) (2011): 81-100.

Levin, B. L. and M. A. Becker, eds. A Public Health Perspective of Women's Mental Health. New York: Springer, 2010.

Martin, R. E., F. Gold, W. Murphy, V. Remple, J. Berkowitz, and D. Money. "Drug Use and Risk of Bloodborne Infections: A Survey of Female Prisoners in British Columbia." *Canadian Journal of Public*

Health/Revue canadienne de santé publique 96 (2) (2005): 97-101.

Richie, B. E. "Challenges Incarcerated Women Face as They Return to Their Communities: Findings from Life History Interviews." *Crime & Delinquency* 47 (3) (2001): 368-389.

Van Den Bergh, B., A. Gatherer and L. F. Møller. "Women's Health in Prison: Urgent Need for Improvement in Gender Equity and Social Justice." *Bulletin of the World Health Organization* 87 (6) (2009): 406.

Van Den Bergh, B. J., A. Gatherer, A. Fraser, and L. Møller. "Imprisonment and Women's Health: Concerns About Gender Sensitivity, Human Rights and Public Health." *Bulletin of the World Health Organization* 89 (9) (2011): 689-694.

I'm An Addict

MELISSA GLOVER

As desperation and hopelessness
rush out with empty hands
and scare my heart and soul,
I know my life is a void.

Addiction runs strong through my veins.
Escape? There is no escape.
If I were free of it all,
where would I go?
what would I do?

Sadness seeps deep through my soul
with waves of fear and loneliness.
I want to be happy, to be loved,
and know what it's like to really love,
but I'm an addict.

I'm lost, searching for a sense
of belonging, of knowing.

I'm an addict.

Child Not Wanted

MO KORCHINSKI

FOR MUCH OF MY LIFE, I have been so full of anger and self-pity that I couldn't feel anything else. My earliest memories are full of fear. Growing up, my bedroom was my safe place, safe from violence. I learned that being alone was safer. Instead of showing anyone that I was hurting, I turned inward. When I was very young, I stopped crying to show that I couldn't be hurt. I learned to stuff my feelings away. I didn't trust anyone, including kids my own age. I stopped caring. I felt I couldn't do anything right, so why try?

When I was eight, we moved to Vancouver Island. My parents bought a corner store with an attached house. The house had only one bedroom. Beside the house was a one room cabin where all three children stayed until the second floor of the house was built. I no longer had a safe place.

People saw that I was not a happy child. Teachers tried to keep me out of more trouble at home by letting me pass classes that I shouldn't have passed because they worried about me. I remember being at our neighbour's house. I went there quite a lot. She loved having a little girl around to do her hair and to help bake. I loved being over there. I was starving for attention.

When I was eleven years old a family member started to sexually abuse me. I had no one that I could turn to, no one I trusted that I could tell. When I would go to bed, I would lie there in fear, not sure when he would come into my room. This went on for several months. I never told anyone that this was going for the fear that I would get blamed. Then I found out I was pregnant. I didn't know what to do. I wrote a letter to my best friend and told her a story that I was walking home from her place one night when it was just starting to get dark when I was grabbed and held down by three guys while another guy raped me and I got away. It was a relief to talk to someone even if the facts of

18

the rape were not the truth. The true facts would never be told; it was something that I thought I would take to the grave with me. I'd been so scared and ashamed, and I felt really dirty. Until writing my story for this book, I have told people the same story that I told my best friend and I have lived with my guilt and shame of the abuse.

My best friend confided in her mom, who took my letter to my mom. In school, I was called down to the principal's office where my mother was waiting. She looked angry. My best friend's mother took me to a doctor, who confirmed that I was pregnant. He booked the abortion, and told me that after it was done, I should come back to see him about getting the pill. Not understanding that he was talking about birth control, I thought, shit, now I have to be on a pill for the rest of my life.

Pot and alcohol provided an escape from my feelings. Alcohol gave me the self-confidence I didn't have before. I could talk to people and do things that I couldn't do before. I also didn't put up with any more shit. I stood up for myself. I was soon kicked out of the house. Pot and alcohol became part of my everyday life.

To support my habit I started selling joints. Almost daily, I broke into my parents' place and stole money and smokes. As far as I was concerned, they owed me, so I didn't care how much I took from them.

When I was eighteen, I moved to Alberta and tried coke for the first time. I met a girl who was a stripper and she said she could get me a job where I could drink and work and get paid good money. After the first night I danced, I couldn't remember even finishing all my shows, but no one said anything, so I thought that was cool. I met my husband in this strip club. He worked as a bartender there and partied as much as I did. We got married. I don't remember much of my wedding. When I was six months pregnant, I quit dancing, but kept drinking. After the baby was born, I didn't know how to love her. My marriage fell apart after two years, and I was pregnant some time later with another man. I drank less this time, but I couldn't stop all together. As soon as I got home from the hospital with my newborn baby, I started drinking worse than before. Later we had another child.

Child welfare started coming around. One day I was at the bar while my oldest daughter was at a neighbour's house and the two youngest children were with their dad. The police came to my house and asked my daughter if I was home, and she said no. They called child welfare and took her to a foster home. When I got home from the bar, I went to the neighbour's to pick up my daughter. I was very angry and smelled of booze. The neighbours called the police. Child welfare didn't take my youngest children, and I was doing everything they told me to do in order to get my oldest back. Still, I didn't stop drinking. I didn't think I had a problem. It was everyone else's fault.

Then I found out my mom had cancer. I sent my two youngest children to stay with their dad and I flew to Nanaimo to stay with my mom for six weeks. I tried to find the love and acceptance I'd been looking for my whole life, but wasn't able to let go or to forgive my mom for all the hurt and pain of my childhood. My ex was granted custody of my two youngest children the day before my mom died.

The night my mom died was my son's second birthday, and I picked up the crack pipe. The numbness seemed to solve all my problems. I no longer had a care in the world. I started to sell drugs, which was more addictive than the drugs. Soon I was known by the police, and I was busted and sentenced to one year in jail.

Jail was like coming home and being locked up. It brought back all the horrible feelings I had as a child. I could handle being left out of society and locked away. I stayed clean inside and started to find a purpose and a common interest with other women. But when it came time for me to leave prison, I couldn't wait to numb those painful feelings again. And that's when the cycle of jail started.

My Story

JOY HAPPYHEART[1]

ICOULD TELL THE STORY of what led me to becoming one of the heaviest poly-substance users I've ever met, and I could also tell a lot about what it's like to hurt and be hurt, to be homeless, psychotic, and without hope, but I won't at this time because this isn't the place for that. At age twenty-four, I ended up in jail for the first time. It wasn't for my initial offence of possessing crack for the purpose of trafficking, but because I couldn't show up for court or my appointments while on probation. That was a result of the chaotic behaviour and lifestyle—consequences of my substance use—and I was jailed because of it. It sucked at first because I was extremely dope-sick coming off the heroin, and I was scared shitless to boot. All that went through my drug-fogged mind was: "Now I've done it. Now I've really done it." After a while, I figured out that prison wasn't that bad, and I actually felt a level of safety there. I couldn't stay out of jail for longer than two weeks at a time, with each imprisonment only lasting a few weeks to a few months. I think I was jailed eleven or thirteen times. They weren't locking me up with the intent of helping me; the system was showing their power over me for using drugs and not fitting within social norms, by saying "You are 'bad' so we'll take another thirty days away from you." Nobody would sit down and suggest otherwise; nobody in there took the time to talk to me to suggest to me that there was another way to live and another way to go about things. There was a six-week wait to see a drug and alcohol counsellor inside; I wasn't even really sure what she or he did. I was frightened—as if I would ever bother going to see this person with the power to do things to me.

Each time I was released, I was determined to continue along my path: pick up my welfare check, my pipe and crack, and head back to the doorway I had come from. After years of revolving in and out, I had deteriorated and was eventually shipped off to the forensics institution

21

to have my head checked out because I was insane on the streets. I was yelling at traffic and people, and running around the streets in bare feet for almost the whole month of February. It was nuts, but when the drugs wore off, I was stable enough to pass the test that said I was sane. So, I was shipped back to prison to teach me another lesson.

[1]Joy Happyheart is a pseudonym.

My Addiction

AMBER CHRISTIE

EVERY TIME I'VE BEEN IN PRISON, I was always segregated due to drug withdrawal. For some reason I don't know, when you are withdrawing from drugs, you aren't allowed any books or paper to write or anything to stimulate yourself mentally.

I struggled for ten years with a hefty heroin and cocaine addiction. I lived on Main and Hastings in Vancouver's east end for many years. I've been in prison many times. Every time was due to my drug use. I have been through the revolving doors of Burnaby Correctional Centre for Women (BCCW) and Surrey Pretrial since I was nineteen years old. My life on the streets of Hastings turned me into a person that I didn't really know. Just to survive and maintain my drug habit, I did things on a daily basis that I told myself as a teen I would never do.

My brief stays in prison would always end up the same way. I would be on remand for two weeks (which meant being off drugs) and get sentenced to thirty days (always in segregation) and then I would be back on the streets. I was given nothing: never a housing list or even a question about where I was going or whether there was anything the system could do to help me.

As my addiction progressed, my crimes got worse, too. I was remanded for six months for two assaults with a weapon. I spent nine days in Vancouver's city cells—a hell of its own! I was in a cell with six other women and only two beds for 24 hours a day for nine days straight.

Superheroes with No Power

JEN FLAVEL

WHEN WE ARE CHILDREN, we are constantly told stories with memorable characters like superheroes, wise old owls, fun young pups, and talking teddy bears. Their beautiful images are painted into the imagination that we try and find some way to make a part of our everyday realities. But that is just not the case in real life. In my story, my superhero didn't come to save the day when the wise old owl robbed me of my innocence, and that fun young pup turned out to be a dirty dog. I found myself sitting up at nights wishing my teddy bear could talk because then maybe she could tell somebody my dirty secrets. Mother Goose turned out to be a heart-broken black sheep and the only fairy tale ending I ever saw was the day somebody came and told me the wise old owl fell out of his tree and into a six-foot grave. I know life is not supposed to be easy, but I'm pretty sure when you are a kid, it is supposed to be carefree and innocent.

At such an extraordinarily young age, sex was introduced to me in such a horrifically pleasant manner. It didn't hurt, it didn't cause me any pain (at the time); I had no idea it was a 'bad thing.' I had no idea that I was being 'violated.' I thought I was being loved in some 'special, secret way'; I was so young and ignorant. Even when really dirty things started happening in the basement of some neighbourhood kid's home, not even for one second did I stop to think there was something wrong with what was going on. (How messed up is that?) Looking back on it now, I think not knowing about these violations of personal boundaries made it so much easier to cross even more. Smoking, getting stoned, drinking, and all before the age of twelve!

Not all my childhood memories were bad. We were taught that love and strength come hand in hand. We were taught that life can still be good and filled with laughter and that there are good times even through hell and heartache. We learned the strength of unity while watching our family rip apart. And most importantly, I learned that even a superhero with no powers and a broken-hearted Mother Goose are human, too, and have their own stories and secrets. That's one of many beautiful lessons I learned over the years: no matter what your status is (parent, child, man, woman), no matter what your race or place in society, we all cry tears, we all bleed red. Sooner or later we all come to realize that life isn't about looking back at the pains of your past, or living in the fear of the future. Instead, it's about knowing that during these hard times, all we have to do is look up.

So now I've taken you from child to pre-teen; well, here is the pre-teen to teens. I was a drunk, a pothead, and a total Queen of the Drama Scene. I used to cut myself just to hurt myself and everyone that might give a fuck about me. I overdosed on pills, constantly threatened to kill myself, and then the next day would merrily trip around my neighbourhood looking for the closest swing set or the best bush to duck behind and hit a blunt. I met and had a variety of great friends, but most of them grew tired of my crazy bullshit. I would move on to the next group, and so on and so on. There aren't many people in my home town I could or still can call a friend to this day. The very few that I do, I cherish deeply.

Moving to Kelowna was supposed to be about new beginnings and starting over, but by that point I was done. Already, at thirteen years old, I was throwing in the towel. I gave in, I said fuck it, and went totally nuts. It was a slow, gradual climb up the drug, party, and sex scene, but once I hit the top of that ride, it only took a split second before I found myself at my first rock bottom. I went from a laid-back (angry), easy-going (dramatic), fun-loving (sarcastic) girl, to some lost empty shell of a 'once was' version of myself. I started smoking crack, then eventually IV drugs, which led to prostitution, which led to the use of more drugs.

My Choices

ANNETTE DUBRULE

EIGHT YEARS AGO, I made the choice to destroy my life. My life was going well. I was a stable mother, housewife, and employee, and I had many family members as well as some friends. I had some partner problems and was unhappy about it, but this was no reason to choose to let drugs enter my life. Still, something led me to do so. My drug addiction came quickly.

In my addiction, I made negative choices and failed myself by neglecting myself and what was important to me. I sunk my name big time with credit. I was a "late drug bloomer." I had means of credit and had many friends to give me tips and ideas for cash money through my credit cards and even checks I was writing. When that ran out, the crime started. I had wonderful friends showing me tons of ways to make money fast. It seemed so easy, and was for the longest time. While supporting my friends' habits with the money and drugs I was bringing in, I had tons of friends. For once in my life, I felt accepted and liked.

I started doing crime on my own because I thought everyone around me was too scared. Today I know they were smarter. My choice of crime was working and I was rolling in the money, but eventually I got "lazy" and that started to catch up with me. I was arrested and let out on a promise to appear. Eventually I went to jail for six months and was let out after my two-thirds. It wasn't long enough.

I was sent to jail for a lengthy twenty-month sentence. It still wasn't long enough because when I was given a Christmas Temporary Absence (TA), I took advantage and escaped. I mostly wanted to find my ex and see where things stood. Can you believe that after everything we had been through and after being incarcerated for approximately six months, my head space was still with this boy? Well, I found him, clean and moved on with his life, a new partner, and doing decent. I actually accepted that and turned myself in.

Tears of Hope

ROSIE JONES[1]

ISTARTED OUT SHOPPING. The white man calls it shoplifting. The money came too easy. From 1985 to 2006, I had been in and out of jail. All my adult life I've been in and out of jail—twenty years! Fourteen years doing the needle. With the first needle I put in my arm, I caught hep C. I played Russian roulette with the needle. My life was so dark and cold. I've shot Talwin to Ritalin to morphine to dillies to jib to heroin, the king of drugs. I lived each day then on death row. I've seen and felt death. For four months I was on the run from the law. I was one hundred pounds, I never knew I was that skinny, I thought I looked good, but I felt ugly inside. The king had control of me. I was at the point of giving up my soul because I had nothing else to sell.

I stood on the hill in Prince George and I wanted to give up life. The only thing that saved me from giving up was crying. I felt my soul leaving me very slowly. I felt cold. I was walking on very thin ice, waiting to fall through. I know deep down that crying saved my life. If I hadn't cried, I would be six feet under. I cried for help, but no one could hear me. Still, people around me saw that my tears were the only hope I had. My tears of hope saved me! The king almost had a queen six feet under. I thank God for being with me in my so-called life.

Now clean for five months in prison, I admit I've been to hell and back. All I had to do was close the door on my coffin. The heroin killed my pain and blurred my vision. When I didn't have the king in me, I staggered, and because I felt nothing but hurt inside me, I made sure I hurt someone else too. If I felt bad, I had to make sure someone else felt bad too.

I've done everything in the crime book, you name it I've done it. I've done smash and grabs, I've robbed, I've sold hot goods, I've been involved with stolen cars. I liked being in front, but I ended up in the back seat, letting the king have anything as long as I had a piece of the king in me. The crime got me nowhere but jail.

[1]Rosie Jones is a pseudonym because we were not able to contact Rosie, now living in the community, to ask if she would like her real name used for her story, which she contributed for publication while she was incarcerated.

Incarceration

MO KORCHINSKI

punishment
punishment?
what a joke!
take me to jail
nothing new
take my freedom
waste of my time
tax payers' money
no hope for change
no relief from pain
need my drugs
to cope with life
hopeless and lost
with only time on my side
counting the sleeps
until I'm on the other side
bus ticket in hand
welfare check to cash
off to find my best friend
only one I can trust
start the cycle
of my addiction again

Lost

MO KORCHINSKI

don't know who I am
not sure I ever did
don't know my past
not sure where to begin
don't know what I dislike
not sure what I like
don't know about this pain
not sure how to cope
don't know what to do
not sure where to run
don't know how to stop
not sure where I am
don't know if I care
not sure
don't know
just lost

Arrival

A positive environment helps people have a positive attitude and especially to have hope, which is what drives us all really, isn't it?

—Brenda Tole, Warden

Paragraphs of Passion

F

My passion is learning new things.

G

I would like to learn more about mental and emotional health. Things like co-dependency, self-esteem, assertiveness, and healthy relationships. I would like to make the most of the time that I must spend here. I feel that by joining the research team I am on my way to a better understanding of myself and the obstacles in my life.

H

My passion is to see an end to the drug war in Canada. Our current drug policies are far more devastating than drug use itself. Drug users need not be criminalized, but accepted, nurtured, guided, and respected as valued citizens.

I

My passion about health is anxiety. I believe a lot of people have anxiety—especially in jail. We handle a lot of issues. A lot of people do not know how to deal with anxiety. I would like to learn and educate myself and others about anxiety and how to address this issue.

J

I am passionate about emotional support systems.

Doctor's Journey

RUTH ELWOOD MARTIN

*T*HE NEW PROVINCIAL CORRECTIONAL CENTRE *for women opened this week. I experienced déjà vu as I walked across the central grass meadow, around which the living cottages are located— the setting reminds me of the children's camp in Scotland where my sisters and I went during the summer holidays. The health-care unit sits at the edge of the meadow, at the top of the crest. It is the most serene clinic that I have ever seen, with big windows and muted colours. Today, I also met the warden, Brenda Tole; she is a slight woman, with piercingly blue eyes and sprightly movements. She talked about wanting to create a therapeutic environment, about correctional staff working collaboratively with the health-care team so that together we can address the medical needs of women in prison. It is so refreshing to meet a personable warden who seems to "get it"! I am anticipating great things.*

—Journal entry

Worldwide, prisons in which maximum security, isolation, and retribution are emphasized tend to worsen incarcerated people's mental and physical health (Fazel and Baillargeon 957), which in turn works against their eventual "rehabilitation" and "(re)integration" into society (Møller, Stöver, Jürgens, Gatherer, and Nikogosian 15). On the other side, correctional officers who work in punitive prisons suffer higher rates of stress and burnout as they struggle to balance the security aspects of their job with the humanity of those whom they are serving (Møller et al. 171-173).

The World Health Organisation (WHO) advised that prisons should adopt a whole prison approach to health promotion, in which staff, inmates, and management work towards promoting healthy living (Møller et al. 15,19). This approach improves the (re)integration of inmates into society following their release, improves prison staff health, and improves a country's overall public health (WHO 3).

If you are a parent with school-aged children, you will have noticed how the school principal greatly influences the overall ethos of a school. In a similar manner, the warden of the prison influences the ethos of the prison, which in turn influences the overall health of the prison (Møller et al. 1). For that reason, management should support and reward wardens who foster a healthy ethos (Møller et al. 3) because, as Brenda Tole, prison warden said, "The person who runs the show is the person who really sets the tone in the institution."

From when the prison doors first opened, Brenda shaped the tone and ethos of this prison. She purposefully nurtured her vision into a reality during her tenure as warden. Mo Korchinski participated with passion in the opportunities offered with ideas of her own, including running a home brewery to proposing hairdryers and sunglasses for the women. Among one of the first women to enter the renovated correctional centre, Mo entered through the gates, her hands and heart shackled by a life of drugs and loss.

REFERENCES

Fazel, S. and J. Baillargeon. "The Health of Prisoners." *Lancet* 377 (9769) (2011): 956-65.

Møller, L., H. Stöver, R. Jürgens, A. Gatherer, and H. Nikogosian. *Health in Prisons. A WHO Guide to the Essentials in Prison Health.* Copenhagen: WHO Regional Office for Europe, 2007.

World Health Organization (WHO). "Declaration on Prison Health as Part of Public Health." Moscow: WHO, 2003.

ACCW

MO KORCHINSKI

driving up
in the cold sheriff's van
handcuffed and shackled
wondering if it will be like
the TV shows
I grew up watching
cold cement block buildings
bars on all the windows
surprise!
driving through the gates
green grass and flowers
bridge with a pond
women riding bikes
walking with dogs
they all seem to be
having so much fun
this can't be the jail
the judge sentenced me to
two years less a day

My Arrival

MO KORCHINSKI

THE SUN SHINES BRIGHT and blazes hot on the cold April day I am transferred to ACCW. Sitting on the cold steel seats handcuffed in the back of the sheriff's van, I look at the world going by, people going on with their lives while mine is like a movie on pause. I slide and bump into the woman beside me as the sheriff's van speeds along the treacherous highway. It seems to be taking forever to get to ACCW. Where is this new prison that we were all being moved to? All I see out the window is old, run-down farmland, surrounded by lush green mountains and rolling hills where grazing cattle roam free. Finally, I see the sign that says Alouette Correctional Centre for Women looming up ahead on the left hand side of the long, winding, country road.

Slowly the large metal gate slides open and the sheriff's van drives through the gate. The outside world is now gone and a new life begins behind a thirty-foot high metal chain link fence with razor sharp barbwire. I climb out of the van, sore and stiff from the long drive, and wait to get the handcuffs off my red raw wrists. As I walk up the ramp to the intake office, I look around in amazement and surprise, thinking this cannot be a prison. In front of me is a pond with a golden brown arched bridge. Glittering green trees and lush plump bushes surround the pond.

The open spaces seem to go on and on, no tall cold cement buildings, but long cabin-style buildings. The buildings are in the shape of a horseshoe and in the middle is a field with a volleyball court. This place reminds me of summer camps I've seen on TV where children run around and have fun in the sun. I stop and listen—no sounds of traffic, just running water like a river, birds chirping, and the wind blowing. The handcuffs are taken off and forms are filled in. No one strip-searches me. The correctional officers smile and joke with us as they hand out our new wardrobe and a key to our cell. Our cells are not cells but rooms with a lock that we locked and unlocked ourselves. Off to health care to get cleared for lice, as the guard gives us a brief tour pointing out the kitchen and the living units Alder, Birch A and B, and Cedar A and B, as well as where the program building is, where we can find the gym and a library. Sandy field with lonely patches of green grass, growing slowly towards the wide open blue sky.

This place is like no prison I've seen before. It is serene. My living unit looks like someone's living room. Sunlight comes pouring through the big windows and large skylights. My bedroom is bright with a large window looking out at the wilderness. There is a bed with a nightstand with a lamp for reading, a desk with a TV sitting on the corner, a closet with shelves to put my clothes on, hangers to hang the clothes. I have a thought, "this is a place where I could do my time standing on my head." I make my bed and put away my clothes feeling a little confused that there is no guard watching over me. I am afforded privacy, and I wander outside to have a smoke and enjoy the peace and quiet of my new surroundings. I am able to simply walk in and out of my living unit without having to buzz a door and get permission.

The difference between this prison and the one I came from, BCCW, is like night and day. BCCW was dark and cold while ACCW is bright and warm. I have freedom and independence to move around. BCCW had many locked doors, which I had to buzz and wait to go through just to come to another locked door. BCCW made me feel like I was a person who needed permission for everything—to breathe, walk, eat, or go to the bathroom. We weren't free to think for ourselves; we were like robots that BC Corrections programmed. We could make no choices for ourselves.

In this new place, we gather in the evening in the kitchen to have supper with all the other women in the prison, like a big family eating together. I see women catch up with each other over dinner; they sit down when and with whomever they like. We socialize with everyone in the prison, not separated from each other like in other prisons. After supper, we watch TV, go to the library to get a book, go to the gym for a game of volleyball, or just hang out. What a difference from BCCW where meals were brought up to our living units on trays and where we ate with just the women who were on our unit, while guards were watching us.

The first night in my new room, I lie in bed thinking about how my life seems to be repeating itself. Locked away from everyone like a child no one wants, I slowly fall asleep.

If you are working with a team and you have respect for each member of the team and you give them the opportunity to express themselves, you know you're not always going to agree, but everybody has the opportunity to put forward their thoughts and be listened to.

—Brenda Tole, Warden

And then [we] asked each woman what their passion was upon joining our team, and it is unbelievable to see the change in women, as they get to learn more about themselves, their "passion," find out ways for them to change or heal, and also realize that they are not alone.

—Debra Hanson, Inmate Research Coordinator

Inside the Warden's Office

INTERVIEW BY RUTH ELWOOD MARTIN

RUTH: *WHAT JOURNEY DID YOU TAKE to be where you are now?*

Brenda: Let me begin with a story about my mother. At one time, she taught physical education in a junior high school and recreation programs in the community. For years, my mother was mostly a homemaker. But then, after being out of the workforce for years, and with no corrections background, she decided to apply for a job as the recreation director at the women's federal correctional institution. Much to my father's fright, my mother got the job. At this time, I was in high school, and on weekends, she took me with her to work. There were no regulations against it at the time. I played badminton and chess and table tennis in the gym with the women, and I never really thought anything about it. Many, many years later when [the new] Fraser Valley Institute was opened, I walked through the same entry gates, and I remembered I had been there when my mom was the recreation director.

Ruth: *Tell me about your decision to go into corrections.*

Brenda: I was actually planning on becoming a physical education teacher, but when I finished my degree, there were few available teaching positions. I noticed a posting for probation officer training and I thought that sounded interesting because I had an interest in social work, too. So I applied and completed the training and started as a probation officer. I stayed for seventeen years and I loved it.

Then I transferred to the custody division to be the director of a work release unit in Surrey. Inmates would get close to the end of their sentences, and they would come out on a Temporary Absence (TA) and they would live in the work release unit under that TA and they would look for a job and also do some community work service. They had a supportive environment to live in while they tried to re-establish themselves in a community. They were encouraged to take programming, and we had good relationships with a number of community organizations.

We then initiated a program of electronic monitoring with an ankle bracelet. If you went to jail for a non-violent offence, and you had a home and a job, you could complete your sentence at home. The ankle bracelet verified that you were in your home when you were supposed to be. Supervisors went to your home to touch base with you to make sure things were going okay. We decided to incorporate the two programs because they fit together very well. These new programs focused on the community, in a more normalized environment. People felt better, did better. It was a very useful, positive, productive, cheap program.

Ruth: *What did the media make of these two programs, work release and electronic monitoring?*

Brenda: At that time [the late 1980s, early '90s] there was an expectation, from our headquarters and from the government, that correctional administrators would talk to local media. If there was an 'incident' and the media phoned, you answered the questions; or, you got the answers, phoned them back, and gave them the answers. But that has since changed. If you can establish a rapport with the local media, the local media will give the good news stories in addition to the bad news stories. You want balance, so the public understands how the work of your correctional institution can benefit from connections with the community, and how this involvement benefits the community, too. Positive media coverage helps build relationships with the community.

Ruth: *Tell me about your move to Alouette Correctional Centre for Women (ACCW).*

Brenda: It was an old male jail: ugly buildings, very old, in poor repair, with beautiful grounds and an ugly fence around it and lots of cross-fencing within it. The site was full of fences. We renovated it. We took the time to find the kind of design that would work best. We wanted to incorporate the knowledge of the people who were going to deliver programs and who were going to work within the structure to tell us what kind of design would work best for them.

The living units have big windows; they have skylights and natural light. There is a living area versus an institutional area. The colour scheme has natural and vibrant colours instead of drab institutional colours. And the women have their own keys and open their own doors. They have some level of privacy and access to the outside.

The women are outside a lot. Physical activity, including walking and running, is encouraged. Getting outside in the fresh air and the sun is very beneficial. Far away from traffic sounds, there are sounds of water, wildlife, and birds. You can open your window in the morning and hear natural sounds. The landscape is spectacular.

The actual physical plant design and centre environment have a significant impact on staff and offenders, particularly those offenders suffering from mental health issues. All women benefit from access to natural light, fresh air, regular physical activity, and non-controlled movement whenever possible. It is also important to note that this type of building is generally much cheaper to build and maintain compared with typical correctional institutions.

Women, particularly Aboriginal women, tend to be classified to higher security levels than required. All offenders, particularly those with mental health disorders, manage much better in a less restrictive and therapeutic setting. When we opened Alouette Correctional Centre for Women, we had an opportunity to slowly move away from a security and control-focused model and towards a more pro-social offender responsibility model. We used a good classification system to place women immediately at the least restrictive setting, which is a more consistent and efficient process, rather than making women later apply for, or earn, this placement.

It is very difficult to move from long standing attitudes and ideas about safety and security. However, we found the normalized environment made the centre safer for staff and inmates, and institutional violence and use of force incidents greatly reduced when compared to other correctional centres for women.

Ruth: *What about the need for segregation?*

Brenda: The use of segregation, other than for serious disciplinary matters, has a very negative effect, in particular on women and those with mental health disorders. I have not seen any benefit from isolating an individual for extended periods from support, comforts, and human contact. If anything, this procedure tends to escalate problem behaviours. What has benefited these people is not isolating them, but rather providing extra staff or contractors to engage with them, and to offer close attention from health professionals.

Ruth: *What concerns guided your decisions about programs at ACCW?*

Brenda: Good health services are one of the most important components of the correctional centre. Physical and mental health professionals who work in co-ordination with Corrections in delivering consistent and timely health services including preventative education are essential. Providing health services to a community standard is an ongoing struggle. There is also the need for continuity of care upon reintegration to the community. Partnerships with provincial health authorities could provide this community standard and continuity of care, and could promote a patient-first /offender-second approach. Staff training from forensic mental health services helps staff understand mental health symptoms and non-compliance behaviours from a different perspective and exposes them to hospital model interventions in dealing with offenders with mental health disorders.

A high percentage of women in custody have dependent children. Women are often in centres that are large distances from their children and families. Initiatives that promote and foster contact between women and their children are beneficial to both, including enhanced visits, email, tapes, telephone calls, and letters. Research shows that the children of women incarcerated are more negatively impacted if the contact with their mother is limited or absent.

One of the most compelling factors for a woman to change her behaviour or life style is pregnancy and then her baby. Having a supportive mother/baby program at Alouette had an amazingly positive impact on the mothers involved, the other inmates, and the staff. Out of thirteen mothers who brought babies back from the hospital and were released to the community with their babies, eleven have remained out of custody. This initiative was a partnership with several other ministries and community agencies and was based on the best interests of the child.

If you expect both staff and inmates to treat everybody with respect and to exercise their responsibilities, people will rise to those expectations and do the right thing, at least most of the time. And that's how you plan and that's how you run it, not on the basis that one percent of the population is going to breach those expectations.

The more we gave people opportunities, the more they valued the opportunities and responded. The more we gave responsibility for doing things to the women themselves, and the more we talked to the staff about our plans, the better the situation got.

Ruth: *Can you give me some examples of the responsibilities you gave to the women?*

Brenda: Well, we gave them the responsibility, with the recreation therapist, to run the inmate committee. They presented the things that they wanted to discuss, they developed the agenda, and they developed resource materials that supported whatever it was that they wanted to discuss. They were respectful and we were respectful to them, and I think that process was quite delightful.

The inmates actually created an orientation for women arriving at the institution. They gave information, put up notices, and were involved in organizing events in the library. The more responsibility they had, the better job they did. It wasn't without problems. People make mistakes—that's part of the reason that they're here—and it's a learning process. So, when things went sideways, we just had a discussion with everybody, put things back on track, and away we went.

Ruth: *Of all the things you could have talked about, you're focusing on the fact that you were actually giving the women more responsibility.*

Brenda: I think it's the same in any environment. If you are working with a team and you have respect for each member of the team and you give them the opportunity to express themselves, you know you're not always going to agree, but everybody has the opportunity to put forward their thoughts and be listened to. The women had brilliant ideas. They came up with things that we hadn't thought of, things that moms would need or would find helpful. You know I thought we were quite thorough, but in reality, the women came up with all kinds of stuff. And they came up with things that helped, like a package of food when people first came and needed that extra nutrition.

I think the more you try to control people and the more rules you place on them, the more resentful and unhappy they become. Then you have problems and a lot more conflict. The more rules and the more control you put in place, the more the staff feels the need to enforce. It isn't an easy process for the correctional staff to let go of control because that's what our business is, and we've learned to do that well.

Ruth: *How did you help the staff come on board?*

Brenda: It was a learning experience for them too. There was a number of quite progressive, interested, dynamic, positive staff. Some staff had been in the system a long time and didn't see this new kind of direction as a good way to go. We did things slowly and gave people time to adjust. We encouraged as much training as we could, and we tried to listen to everybody's concerns. Over time we moved. We really noticed how far we'd moved when we had lateral transfers of staff to ACCW from other institutions.

We started doing things like the baby program, the health forums, and making community connections. The staff and the contractors worked together and involved the women in decision making. The rest of the management team was quite supportive. They could see that the environment was probably less dangerous than it had ever been at BCCW. There were fewer instances of violence, and there was no self-harm to speak of, and there was a minimal use of segregation. Open communication with staff and administration can reduce the development of the negative subculture often operating in a correctional centre. Offenders should be encouraged to take responsibility for appropriate aspects of centre operations with the supervision of staff.

Ruth: *Do you have statistics for those three years?*

Brenda: There was no escape attempt. There was no staff assault. There was no use of force. There was no use of an extraction team. If the women had to be moved from one place to another, they just walked. There was the withdrawal of use of restraints for anybody who was expecting. Self-harm is a very complex and difficult issue, but in four years at ACCW there were no suicides and only one minor incident of self-harm.

Ruth: *Any advice for creating prisons that are healing?*

Brenda: The women need good health care and they need opportunities for physical exercise and working outside in the fresh air. They need to be involved in planning and organizing events in their lives. And they need opportunities to connect with the community. Also, because the women come from all over the province, they're so separated, they're so isolated from their families. The ideal situation would be to house women close to the community; if you can't do that, then maybe house them in a place like ACCW for a short time and then move them into facilities in the community.

If you look at any institution, the flavour of that institution and the view of that institution are reflected by the person that has the most empowerment. It's not always the wardens—sometimes it's the director of operations or someone in another management position. The person who runs the show is the person who sets the tone. If the warden is running the show, then their basic principles and their philosophy are going to be reflected. And I don't know how you get around that, other than you pick the people. You can't mandate compassion.

Ruth: *So, is that the key? Compassion?*

Brenda: I think it is. And respect, that's the other thing. Mutual respect between staff and offenders is critical for a safe and secure centre. Staff who engage offenders with respect and are focused on being professional and helpful contribute to an environment that is pro-social. A better working environment affects staff recruitment and retention and lowers rates of staff absences. The positive aspects of good staff and offender relations are seen in inmates' program interest and participation.

There are lots of things that could happen. But it takes will and recognition among the people who make the decisions about prisons. It is possible to create prisons with a positive environment for the staff and inmates. A positive environment helps people to have a positive attitude and especially to have hope, which is what drives us all really, isn't it?

Daily Life

Many women were never taught how to live life, things that so many people take for granted in the outside world. Things that come naturally to others by being taught as children, so many women never had those chances to learn and be nurtured by loving parents.

—Mo Korchinski

Paragraphs of Passion

K

My passion is being creative, especially sewing, I really enjoy that. I used to sew all my clothes and my children's clothes. I would like to get my life in order, not shoplift, support myself, and not resort to crime. I do not want to return to jail.

L

I'm so glad to get a chance to help.

M

Women need to learn how to communicate, look for employment, manage life. The first step is to be honest with not only yourself but employers, family, friends. If you are honest about yourself and the mistakes you've made, chances are people will respect you for that. I have learned this.

N

I have good computer skills and plan on sharing my skills and ideas with the research team.

O

I would like to better my life spiritually, physically, and mentally through staying clean, one day at a time. I want to learn about myself, as well as about others who are addicted or recovering from alcohol and drugs.

P

I am interested in breast cancer, ovarian and uterine cancer. I had a hysterectomy at twenty-two because of first stage cancer. Cancer affects many people. I would like to learn more about the hereditary aspects.

Doctor's Journey

RUTH ELWOOD MARTIN

I ARRIVED LATE THIS MORNING for work (which isn't unusual!). I don't usually share personal information, but, for some reason today, I explained that I was late because I drove my son to work. The women asked, "What work does your son do?" I explained that he had a summer job as a lawn cutter. There was a puzzled pause among the group of women, and then one asked me, "But, Dr. Martin, why is your son cutting lawns? Surely, you have enough money that he doesn't need to cut lawns!" I explained that my son was hoping to study at university and that he needed a summer job to help to cover his expenses. The women then started discussing their own childhood. I sat back and listened. One woman described how her mother had taught her to steal at the age of ten when they went shopping; her mother would beat her if she did not wheel a shopping buggy containing a large appliance out of a department store. Another woman, with tears streaming down her cheeks, told us that she stole new toys for her child, but, when she resumed her addiction, she would wait until her son fell asleep at night to pawn his new toy so that she could buy drugs. In the morning, her child would cry because he couldn't find his new toy. One woman told us that she had recently taken a budgeting course; she learnt about the price of groceries, and how to plan ahead for paying rent and hydro. Then, together, the women agreed that they wanted to learn all this: to learn about living and working without drugs and without crime—and, to learn "the value of the dollar, like Dr. Martin's son."

— Journal entry

Female prisoners are outnumbered by male prisoners (90 percent of Canadian prisoners are male), and the needs of incarcerated women throughout the world tend to be subsumed by correctional policies that are designed for men (Van Den Bergh; Corston.) In addition, female

56

criminal pathways have direct or indirect links to trauma history, which begs for gender sensitive and therapeutic correctional settings for incarcerated women (Van Den Bergh et al.).

During this project, incarcerated women gave voice to a host of ideas that would enhance their health, including improved peer and community support and safe and stable housing (Martin et al. 2009a, 2009b). We learned that incarcerated women are relational and they yearn for healthy mentors (Martin, Chan, Torikka, Granger-Brown, and Ramsden).

This chapter gives voice to stories of women in prison who were living in ways that included caring for each other, mentoring each other, and learning from each other. Women in prison were learning how to live life in a world that was not centred on crime and substance use; they were learning how to live everyday life.

REFERENCES

Corston, J. "The Corston Report. A Review of Women with Particular Vulnerabilities in the Criminal Justice System." 2007. Web.

Martin, R., R. Chan, L. Torikka, A. Granger-Brown, and V. R. Ramsden "Healing Fostered by Research." *Canadian Family Physician* 54 (2008): 244-245.

Martin, R. Elwood, K. Murphy, R. Chan, V. R. Ramsden, A. Granger-Brown, A. C. Macaulay, R. Kahlon, G. Ogilvie, and T. G. Hislop. "Primary Health Care: Applying the Principles Within a Community-based Participatory Health Research Project that Began in a Canadian Women's Prison." *Global Health Promotion* 16 (4) (2009b): 43-53.

Martin, R. Elwood, K. Murphy, D. Hanson, C. Hemingway, V. Ramsden, J. Buxton, A. Granger-Brown, L. L. Condello, M. Buchanan, N. Espinoza-Magana, G. Edworthy, and T. G. Hislop. "The Development of Participatory Health Research Among Incarcerated Women in a Canadian Prison." *International Journal of Prisoner Health* 5 (2) (2009a): 95-107.

Van Den Bergh, B. "Women's Health in Prison: Urgent Need for Improvement in Gender Equity and Social Justice." *Bulletin of the World Health Organization* 87 (6) (2009): 406-406.

Van Den Bergh, B. J., A. Gatherer, A. Fraser, and L. Moller. "Imprisonment and Women's Health: Concerns About Gender Sensitivity, Human Rights and Public Health." *Bulletin of the World Health Organization* 89 (9) (2011): 689-694.

A Day in the Life of Prison

MO KORCHINSKI

A T ACCW, EVERYONE IN THE PRISON has a job. Most women work
on the horticulture work crew, others in the kitchen, laundry room,
or cleaning. When I arrived, there was a lot of work on the horticulture
crew because the prison's landscaping was not finished. The seed was
planted for the grass, which needed to be watered and kept wet. There
were trees and bushes to prune and flowerbeds needing to be built. We
were asked for our input in the plans of the landscaping and what we
would like to see happen. Our opinions mattered.

For most women the day started at 6:30 a.m. After breakfast, women
went back to the living units to tidy up. Women worked from 8:00 a.m.
till 3:30 p.m., and after that, there is free time and dinner.

The weekend was free time for all the women except kitchen staff
whose days off varied. On the weekend, women slept in and had brunch.
Relationships between the women were like those in a family. There
were always one or two women on each unit who played the role of a
mother, guiding the younger ones on basic life skills, like how to clean
their room and to keep good hygiene. I found that many women were
never taught how to live life, things so many people take for granted in
the outside world. Things that come naturally to others by being taught
as children, so many women never had those chances to learn and be
nurtured by loving parents.

At the Inmate Committee Meetings I really understood what was going on, what was happening in the prison (e.g., the canteen lists, the need for hairdryers) and what was going wrong. We couldn't fix everything, but the interaction was really good for me and helped me understand.

—Brenda Tole, Warden

The hardest proposal for me to get passed was getting sunglasses. There was a big debate about how the guards wouldn't be able to see our eyes. As most women worked outside in the sun, I felt that UV rays were very harmful to our eyes. I wouldn't give up. Not sure what the security issues were, but for some reason sunglasses were not allowed. But it made no sense, since we were promoting sunscreen and covering up from the sun.

—Mo Korchinski

Flashback 1: Life in Prison
(Win2H meeting, November, 2010)

"THANKS FOR COMING. We thought we'd get together, and talk about the things in prison that we liked. You know, some of the events, what you remember, things that made you laugh. So, let's start with diet and building the vegetable gardens."

"When I first went to prison in 2004, one of the first things that I noticed was all the bread women are fed. When women started to complain about the unhealthy eating habits and all the weight that comes from eating way too much bread, we took this concern to our monthly inmate coordinators meeting."

"I couldn't believe how much weight I put on! None of the clothes I was wearing when I came into prison fit when I left. I had to stuff myself into my jeans."

"It was a real downer."

"I couldn't believe how much work we had to do."

"Most of us worked in the horticulture program."

"Yeah, we were responsible for taking care of the grounds inside and outside the prison."

"Remember how we started our own vegetable garden, right from scratch, building the raised flower beds, to hauling wheelbarrows of dirt to fill them?"

"Yeah! My arms ached for days!"

"The prison had one greenhouse building and one cold shed where we learned how to start vegetable and flowers from scratch. We sure worked hard together—the entire horticulture crew—and soon the flower beds were ready to plant."

"We had so many different vegetables."

"Lettuce, peas, corn, beans, tomatoes."

"And a variety of herbs, I didn't know half of them!"

"They added a healthier flavour to our meals."

"It was fun watching everything grow. I will never forget this, everyone had so much fun. Everyone was so happy!

"Yeah, but it sure sucked when it rained."

Putting Responsibility into the Women's Hands
Inmate Committee Meeting

MO KORCHINSKI

ONE OF THE INITIATIVES in ACCW was the Inmate Committee Meeting. Traditionally, Corrections see inmate meetings as potential for trouble. They want to control the agenda to reduce inmates' power. Each living unit rep worked with Alison (the recreation therapist) to come up with the agenda for the meetings. I became the "inmate coordinator" and planned for a monthly meeting with the wardens and staff to bring to the table ideas women had for the prison. With the unit reps, I would put together the agenda for each month's meeting. Alison would facilitate the meeting. All the white shirts (wardens) and two people from each living unit would meet once a month. Women would come up with some ideas for change and put together proposals and we would all sit down and discuss them as equals—not Corrections versus inmate.

We brought many different issues to the table. We talked openly about each item on the agenda and why we thought we should have something or change something. The wardens would offer their ideas and we would give ours. Most of the time, the warden would ask us to provide research to back up our ideas.

Our opinion mattered. Our voices were heard. It was the difference between earning respect and demanding respect from us. If after a good discussion, the result was "no," then there was a good reason for it and in that case the women accepted the decision. The meetings created a culture that supported healthy collaboration and communication.

Among the things we first requested were hair dryers and curling irons. I remember saying in the proposal that having wet hair causes women to get sick but, apparently, that is a myth. So, the next monthly meeting we redid the proposal and came up with the reason that if we look good, we feel good, and when we feel good, we are happier. And we got the hair dryers and curling irons for each unit.

ACCW was open to change and the women took pride in their surroundings. A community was starting to form inside the walls of the prison.

We put in proposals to have events where women could have fun and come together as a community. One of the biggest complaints from many women was our diet. People coming off drugs need a high carb diet, but eating so many carbs led to women putting on lots of weight. This gave us an idea of how to incorporate exercise with fun: sports day. This was out first big event. Learning to have fun and finding my inner child that was lost for so many years was so new to me. I laughed and felt content with who I was becoming, and I saw what life can be like without drugs and other substances to numb me. This event was a big success, and we started to plan other weekend events.

After most of the landscaping was done around the grounds of the prison, we also thought about growing fresh vegetables for healthy eating instead of having bread all the time. The prison bought two greenhouses where we started to grow vegetable plants from seed, and learned how to nurture and care for them. We took pride in what we were doing and we enjoyed the vegetables. We also built thirty raised flower beds. We hauled many wheelbarrows with dirt to fill the beds as well as wheelbarrows with gravel to fill in the pathways. Lots of hard work but the result was so worth it: fresh vegetables.

To help raise money for the Inmate Committee, we put on a barbeque where women could buy hotdogs and hamburgers. We made a large home-grown salad as a side dish, a nice treat compared to eating the food that we served every day in the kitchen.

We did more barbeques, scavenger hunts, volleyball tournaments, and Easter egg hunts when women ran around the prison grounds trying to find eggs. Even the crows in the air joined the hunt, flapping around with shiny, foil-wrapped, and coloured eggs in their beaks.

The more we gave people opportunities, the more they valued the opportunities and responded. The more we gave responsibility for doing things to the women themselves, and the more we talked to the staff about our plans, the better the situation got.

—Brenda Tole, Warden

Most of us only knew happy and angry, all the feelings in between were foreign to us. ACCW wouldn't punish women for coming out sideways, but would help women to get through our issues.

—Mo Korchinski

Working Things Out

MO KORCHINSKI

LIKE EVERY COMMUNITY, we had our problems, but the way these problems were handled was different from other prisons. For example, there was a woman I knew from the streets and I'd had a problem with her for many years. One day we were arguing and she called me a goof and I got up and punched her. To most people the word "goof" is no big deal, but inside prison "goof" is a term reserved for child molesters. Other inmates beat goofs in prison, so if you don't defend yourself when you're called a goof, people look at you and think that because you took it dry, there must be a reason why.

I was sentenced to fifteen days in segregation. I was locked in a cell for twenty-three hours a day, isolated from everyone else. While in segregation the recreation therapist, Alison Granger-Brown, and two correction officers came in and did a restorative justice process with both of us. Spending time locked away from everyone gives you time to think and reflect on your behaviour. The other woman and I solved our problems while in segregation, and we were okay with each other by the time we were let out after fifteen days.

Finding a solution to the bigger problem was a new concept at ACCW, so different from the way things were handled at BCCW. When women were released from segregation, there was peace, which in turn kept peace with everyone in the prison. Friends didn't have to get involved as there was nothing to get involved with.

When women were having a problem with each other, they would be invited to restorative justice so that they could talk about what was going on and come to some kind of peace. For most of the women, the answer to problems is to fight—it's a way of life for many of us who come from the world of addiction. But when we are treated like equals, we learn new ways of communicating.

Most of us only knew happy and angry, all the feelings in between were foreign to us. It can be very overwhelming once these feelings start to surface. Not understanding what is happening, our moods can be unpredictable. ACCW wouldn't punish women for coming out sideways, but would help them get through issues. Instead of someone going into segregation, isolated from everyone else, the prison would get women to clean windows and other extra jobs around the grounds. The prison was not a typical prison; it felt like a healing lodge. Women started to feel safe and slowly started to put down the guards they had built up around themselves. We took a look at ourselves.

Some women didn't want to leave because they weren't ready to go back to life on the streets. They were experiencing inner healing. ACCW for many of us was a safe healing centre. The biggest challenge was how to integrate women back into society with the same feeling of safety.

Flashback 2: Life in Prison
(Win2H meeting, November, 2010)

"I remember working with the dogs. Remember? We would bring the dogs inside and foster them from the local SPCA. Nothing is more healing than waking up with a dog in your bed. It was a huge bonus."

"I loved doggy daycare!"

"It really helped me a lot."

"Having the dogs made me focus on the dogs instead of myself. It helps you to socialize."

"When you're locked up, it makes such a difference to have a dog with you in the room—you can talk to him and not feel as lonely."

"Hey! Do you remember Chase?"

"Which one was he?"

"You know, the cross breed who needed surgery because he was born with a deformed paw and—"

"Oh, right! I remember him!"

"There was no money to get it fixed."

"Right, so we started selling cartons of ice cream from Save-On Foods who gave us a great deal on the price to help our cause."

"Once a week we'd take ice cream orders, which cost $5 a carton."

"That was half my weekly wage!"

"Yeah, right, but we wanted to help Chase."

"And we'd put the profit into a special account to pay for Chase's surgery."

"Remember how supportive the staff were on helping us raise the money? They'd haul a truck load of ice cream in the back of the pickup truck."

"I wasn't in there then. How long did you do it for?"

"We did this for three months!"

"And the surgery was successful!"

"This fundraiser gave us women a purpose to make a difference. For many of us giving back to a worthy cause was something new."

*All these events taught me what a community is
and how you can build a community anywhere.*
—Mo Korchinski

*If things go sideways,
we talk it over,
reflect on what
we might do
differently,
and move forward.*
—Brenda Tole, Warden

Ground Rules

MO KORCHINSKI

L ike all prisons, drugs can be a problem, but here, inmates were angry whenever drugs came into the prison. The feeling of healing was so strong that women didn't want that life of the outside world to come inside. We had so much to lose inside. With all the trust and respect between inmates and correctional staff, we didn't want to lose it. To show respect to the Aboriginal Elder Holy Cow and the recreation therapist Alison Granger-Brown, who both went beyond the call of their jobs to help make ACCW what it was, mattered to us. Women didn't want to let them down, we wanted their respect.

There is a saying inside prison: "gay for the stay, straight at the gate." Women who never looked at women in a sexual way seemed to form relationships with each other while behind the walls of prison. This caused many problems between staff and inmates, but most of these relationships weren't sexual, but more about cuddling and holding hands or just feeling loved. Depending on who was working, there were different sets of rules about what was allowed between two women. This, too, caused friction for staff and inmates. So, we had a meeting with the warden, Brenda Tole, the inmate coordinator, guards, unit reps, and Alison. We needed to come up with guidelines for what was acceptable and what wasn't. Which way to hold hands, with fingers locked together or cupping each other's hands in plain sight? How long should a kiss be, just a quick peck on the lips or one, two, or three seconds? The meeting didn't go well. A few correctional guards who thought that there should be zero tolerance for any kind of relationship between inmates walked out of the meeting. Yet, we did end up with a joint set of rules to be followed by all the staff and the women.

Flashback 3: Life in Prison
(Win2H meeting, November, 2010)

"Remember the Running Club with Alison?"

"That was my favourite program!"

"Yeah, Alison would take us on hikes and then we got the bikes."

"Where'd the bikes come from anyway?"

"The Inmate Committee and the jail split the cost half and half and got us ten bikes. The women who couldn't go on the running club could still ride the bikes around the jail."

"Yeah that was my job one summer—keeping up on the repairs of the bikes. That was neat!"

"I liked the running club because it gave me a false illusion that I wasn't in jail any more, just going for a bike ride or out at the park like a normal person on a sunny day."

"Just to go out for a bike ride or a hike outside the gates was a wonderful change from the confinement of the prison walls."

Business as Usual

MO KORCHINSKI

IN PRISON, YOU CAN'T JUST GO TO THE STORE when you need something. If you ran out of smokes, you had to wait until canteen day, which was on a Tuesday afternoon after work. A couple days before canteen day, most women had run out of tobacco. Imagine being in one place with a hundred women, all bitchy because they craved a smoke? I started up an in-prison cigarette business, so that women could always get a smoke when they needed one. I had a two for one smokes deal, meaning if you got one smoke off me, you would pay me back two smokes, and on canteen day, three for one.

Making homemade brew was another thing I did. First I needed a connection to someone in the kitchen to help me get the stuff to make the homemade brew. Then I needed to find a place to hide the brew while it was maturing. This might seem easy but it's not, as the staff do daily security checks around the grounds of the prison. I also had to take into consideration the security cameras in the control room.

It wasn't just about enjoying the brew; it was also about selling the brew to other women to make extra canteen money. I could sell one water bottle of homemade brew for a large pouch of tobacco. Tobacco is money in prison; tobacco buys whatever you need: make-up, food, drugs, and homemade brew.

I was more addicted to the lifestyle of selling than the actual drugs, and it would sneak up on me when I had nothing to fill my head with other things.

Recreation Therapy

I learned that my role in the prison is to hold the hope for the women.

—Alison Granger-Brown, Recreation Therapist

Paragraphs of Passion

Q

I would like to learn about mental illness and addiction and learn what I put in my body and how I can change.

R

I enjoy crocheting and anything therapeutic to show all women in this place that there has to be a different way to heal themselves on their road to recovery. Anything therapeutic is my forte.

S

My passion is to develop a productive atmosphere for the women in prison in all areas. I believe activities are an essential part of a woman's personal development, rehabilitation process, and road to recovery. A variety of opportunities to choose from is key to making every woman's time in prison beneficial, productive, healthy, and positive.

T

My passion is empowering women through education in health and fitness, which incorporates nutrition, physical fitness, and self-empowerment strategies. I would like to learn about how nutrition and fitness can assist in recovery from addictions.

U

My passion is eating disorders and the personal experience of women suffering or who have suffered from eating disorders.

V

I would like to learn more about emotional abuse and "borderline personality disorder." I think some women end up in impossible relationships that wear them down and degrade them, but because the man doesn't actually physically beat them, they consider themselves lucky. I think this research would help myself and many women understand themselves and their relationships better.

Doctor's Journey

RUTH ELWOOD MARTIN

*T*ODAY, *ALISON GRANGER-BROWN, the prison recreation therapist, and I had one of our kindred spirit meetings in the prison car park. We both work incredibly long hours, and we tend to meet each other in the evening as we are both going out of the gates. We chatted about sleep and ways that women in prison can (re)discover how to fall asleep without using substances. "Why do prison physicians tend to prescribe night-time medications for the women?" she asked me. Alison is growing herbs with the women, so that the women can drink chamomile tea before going to bed. She takes groups of women out into the community for cross-country running. She is also teaching them yoga and relaxation exercises. Our chat then veered onto brain neurotransmitters, the role of oxytocin in nurturing and mother-child bonding.*

—Journal entry

Imprisonment lifts women out of the chaos of substance use and crime, homelessness, and violence: some women see imprisonment as an opportunity for health and learning. One of the health goals collectively voiced by women in prison during the prison participatory health research project was to learn how to live healthily—how to integrate healthy living into their everyday life.

The World Health Organization calls for the creation of prisons as healthy settings (Møller et al. 15-20) but, sadly, a prison environment is not necessarily conducive to learning how to live healthily. Dissonance exists between the concept of prisons as healthy settings and the reality of the correctional mandate to provide a secure environment. For example, Nick de Viggiani, author of an ethnographic study in a UK prison, challenges the notion of a "healthy prison" as something of an oxymoron unless significant reform occurs in the management of prisons and the treatment of incarcerated individuals. The study revealed a range of deprivation and importation factors related to the regime and structured environment of the prison (de Viggian 129-131). Another example is an occupational needs assessment of inmates conducted in a New Zealand large maximum security prison using participation observation, semi-structured interviews with inmates and staff and documentation review. The study's findings, that inmates experienced profound occupational deprivation due to the rigid security policies, were incongruent with the correctional centre's public mission: "to respect the dignity of all individuals ... and the potential for human growth and development as well as preparing inmates for effective reintegration into the community upon their release" (Whiteford 129).

In addition to the impact of the correctional context, many incarcerated women also experience intrinsic barriers to health and learning because of decreased working memory, acute withdrawal from substance use, learning disabilities, fetal alcohol spectrum disorder, attention deficit hyperactivity disorder, post-traumatic stress disorder and other mental health issues.

Alison Granger-Brown delivers therapeutic recreation inside the prison. Therapeutic recreation in prison engages and empowers transformative learning and healing; it attends to the individual learning style; it is a program that is fun and creative; and, it increases motivation for change. Through Alison, I have learnt that therapeutic recreation is a purposive intervention to increase functioning in any of six domains: social, spiritual, cognitive, emotional, creative, and physical. Therapeutic recreation is founded on the principles of "psychosocial integration" (Erikson 1993, 1968), that is, the state in which people flourish as individuals and as members of their culture. Therapeutic recreation creates opportunities for joy and healing as ways of living. These ways of living are vital to replacing addictions and anti-social/ unhealthy behaviours. (William Osler Health System).

The following narratives bear witness to the profoundly healing influence that therapeutic recreation programs have on prison life, on the lives of incarcerated women and, secondarily, on the lives of men and women who worked there.

REFERENCES

Erikson, E. *Childhood and Society.* New York: W.W. Norton and Company, Inc., 1993.

Erikson, E. *Identity, Youth and Crisis.* New York: W. W. Norton and Company, Inc., 1968.

Møller, L., H. Stöver, R. Jürgens, A. Gatherer, and H. Nikogosian, eds. Health in Prisons: A WHO Guide to the Essentials in Prison Health. 1st ed. Copenhagen: World Health Organization-Europe, 2007.

de Viggiani, N. "Unhealthy Prisons: Exploring Structural Determinants of Prison Health." *Sociology of Health & Illness* 29 (1) (2007): 115-35.

Whiteford, G. "Occupational Deprivation and Incarceration." *Journal of Occupational Science* 4 (3) (1997): 126-130.

William Osler Health System. "What is Therapeutic Recreation?" n.d. Web.

Alison's Office

MO KORCHINSKI

ALISON'S OFFICE WAS THE FIRST PLACE I went when I came back to ACCW, with all the large fluffy pillows around the room and the scent of incense lingering in the air. I had many laughs and many tearful talks in this office—it was a safe place to let your emotions out. Alison never judged and always believed in all of us women and would love us because most of us couldn't love ourselves. She taught us how to find our inner self and be okay with what we saw. I remember learning how to be okay with relaxing with the group rest and relaxation she taught every week. The lights would be on low, mats on the floor with the large fluffy pillows under my head, the smell of incense and sound of music.

Some of us joined the running club, which meant you could leave prison to go on walks in the neighbourhood or along the river, through the park, or in the woods around the prison grounds. After we came back from the running club, we would make fresh homemade tea from the plants that we picked on our long exhilarating hikes through the back mountain trails around the prison. Fresh-picked, plump, ripe berries were made into thirst-quenching smoothies, a simple but welcome treat.

Aromatherapy was new for most women. We learned to make soap so we could enjoy some self-pampering after a long day working in horticulture. We would make soap for all the women for their Christmas stockings or just a little something to give a woman on her birthday.

Mask-making was a fun but insightful way to look into your soul and see the beauty that is there, even if it has lost its brightness. A friend applied strips of plaster to my face and then, when the plaster was dry, I painted the outside of the mask, creating my outer beauty in colours that represent me as the loving, caring person I hope to become again.

Just watching as everyone's mask came together, I was struck by the unbelievable creativity of most women. Alison and ACCW gave us love, and with that, hope.

Flashback 4: Life in Prison
(Win2H meeting, November, 2010)

"Hey, do you remember the Easter egg hunts?"

"Every Easter, Alison would bring us an Easter bunny outfit and I'd always pick someone to wear it 'cause I never wanted to, and then three or four of us would go around and hide Easter eggs. We'd get the women to stay locked on their units and then we'd have Control [Operations Control Centre] announce the hunt is on and let everyone out at the same time."

"It was a mad rush. Women running around trying to find chocolate."

"It was funny. You'd watch the crows flying around, stealing the eggs. They were better than some women at finding eggs."

"I remember months later finding eggs hidden in the gardens when I was weeding."

Dropping by the Recreation Therapist's Office

ALISON GRANGER-BROWN

WHEN BRENDA TOLE WAS APPOINTED THE WARDEN for ACCW, she set about familiarizing herself with the staff and the unique nature of a women's prison. She had a wide variety of experience in Corrections from probation to running Vancouver City jail. She had also managed the electronic monitoring program. These earlier experiences gave her a solid understanding of who can be managed outside of the fence—she realized that most women are only a safety threat to themselves. From the beginning of ACCW we felt we had a huge opportunity to create, with the women and staff, a safe and healthy setting that was healing for the women, and that would allow staff to come to work without the often toxic energy that a prison so often inflicts on all those inside the fence. I had the wonderful opportunity to develop and manage my own strategies and approaches to support the women on their healing journey, and doing so, I developed a strong alliance with Brenda as our perspectives in this area were closely aligned.

A prison is by its nature a controlled and structured environment and this included seeing a drug and alcohol counsellor or seeking medical advice. It could take a week or more for the women to get the help they needed, and so the Chaplain and I had open-door policies. We found that simply listening and validating the women's distress or helping them through an immediate crisis of fear or anger could alleviate the pressure on the stretched services and frequently avoided an escalation of the issue. I had large pillows and mats for yoga classes and tried to create a comfortable and safe energy in the room, as building relationship and trust is the essence of helping and of dynamic security.

We tried to be responsive to the most pressing issues of the time and this of course changed with the seasons. For example, Christmas is a very hard time especially for mothers who are separated from children. For many women, Christmas also brings to the fore unpleasant memories associated with their childhood in dysfunctional families. We found ways to celebrate while not ignoring the painful memories but working through them so that every event or project had growth and development opportunities for each individual involved.

Halloween was a wonderful opportunity to nurture creativity. Our events were set up in the gym (doors locked until the appointed hour) and the only supplies were recycled wrapping paper, tissue and newspaper, masking tape, paint, and a few other glittery supplies. I couldn't swear to it but I think a few sanitary supplies snuck in for padding and Santa beards. The imagination was astounding and the simple healthy fun was intoxicating. Everything we designed was inclusive and we would try to engage people who are often marginalized or ostracised in a prison.

Some women were coming in terribly malnourished and were stealing food; this caused much stress. We organized the inmate committee to fund quick cooking porridge, fixed with milk powder for extra calcium, and cinnamon and brown sugar to help the drug cravings. We gave this out when women arrived. It was a sound alternative to the starchy nutritionally poor white bread and margarine.

We decided to take on the sleep medications and started to grow our own chamomile and mint for tea our own version of "Sleepytime" and even our own stevia to sweeten it. This was hugely popular among women, many of whom had never liked herbal teas in the past. We also had ginger and fennel for women struggling with nausea from being drug sick or other reasons. Everything was focused on teaching a more natural and simpler way of satisfying needs. Anything we made or cooked was from scratch and was a platform for teaching budgeting and healthier eating habits.

The more responsibility the women took on for planning and organizing the events, the better they became.

The setting for ACCW was perfect, quiet and hidden in forests and beside a spawning river. I had been taking women out running at BCCW. We expanded this program. I was able to take up to seven women at a time every afternoon for an hour. We brought bikes for women with physical limitations. Off we went up the hill and all around, hiking in the forest, sensing the animals and feeling the fresh air, re-connecting to nature and taking a moment for quiet time.

There were times when we picked enough blackberries for the whole prison to have special pancakes on Sunday. It was a lot of work, but we brought happiness to others. Giving back to the community became very important to the women. For example, after the tsunami in Thailand, the women made dozens of fabric teddy bears from material scraps, which a trucking company helped sell. The money we raised was doubled by the government and we contributed $1,500 to the relief efforts. The teddy bears that did not sell went to Sunny Hill Children's hospital. One of the women who helped make them went with me on a temporary absence to give them to the children who would be in hospital over Christmas.

The inmate committee also sold ice cream to the women and the money we made was used to help with the medical costs for a dog that had been rescued. I have often said that when a woman begins to look outside herself and wants to help for the simple pleasure of helping, I know she is on the road to healing. Altruism is a gift to others and to ourselves. I believe it to be a crucially important part of the ethos of a prison.

We tried various interventions to address criminogenic risk factors in a fun way to encourage the women to try new things to grow and change and realize that they could hope for a healthy, drug-free and crime-free life. For example, we did hip-hop classes as a way to get moving, which entertained the volunteers and visitors!

Having had the experience of a prison healing and learning community, I am committed to creating moments of this in the federal setting and to inspiring others to follow this way, helping the wider community to understand that this is the way to restore balance and healing for the whole community. The validity of this approach is borne out by the lack of self-harm (only one incident in nearly four years), a decrease in aggression, no use of force necessary, and in more than one woman a decrease in mental health issues when placed in the higher security federal setting.

I came to see the prison as a learning community and developed a model for the delivery and facilitation of learning and knowledge acquisition. It attends to the complex needs and learning styles and difficulties of this adult population in a setting that is itself a barrier to learning. The first model attempts in simple terms to describe the individual woman and the stages through incarceration and growth in learning skills and information. The second places this individual in the setting of a prison, or what I prefer to call a correctional learning community. It describes a way to attend to the vast array of learning needs and abilities through a self-directed learning approach so as to teach the women how to resource themselves with information for the rest of their lives. I have argued for this by saying that when a new drug arrives on the streets, the women will learn very quickly how to use it, where to get it, and what sort of high it will give them. They are good learners; our job is to hone the skills and channel them in a positive and pro-social direction.

My role is simply to hold the hope for the women until they can believe in the possibility for healing and begin to hold their own hope. I have learned that hope looks different for everyone and that honouring this is the only way I can stay healthy and remain hopeful regarding the purpose and engagement of my time inside the fence. This is how healing unfolds: first we encourage ourselves to believe, and from there we offer our deepest presence, with unconditional respect for the journey of others, always with gentle honesty, without imposing our ideals, beliefs, and traditions. I know that each person holds within everything she needs to heal, grow, and change. I have learned that my well-being and that of the women and other staff are inextricably linked, and so as we sentence prisoners to hard times, so too we sentence staff to hard times.

Flashback 5: Life in Prison
(Win2H meeting, November, 2010)

"I remember Alison telling me the story behind the labyrinth. When they were touring the grounds of ACCW before it was opened, they went and looked at the fisheries next door, and there was a huge pile of broken tiles and Alison thought they were too nice to throw away, she wanted them. That's when she came up with the idea to haul them all over in the truck over to the jail to build a labyrinth. There was a crew from horticulture that built it with Alison."

"How many tiles did we paint and put into place?"

"Hundreds!"

"A lot of women would write names of people who had passed away or that they've lost to help them deal with their grief and loss. That was part of the teachings of the labyrinth of garden, taking time to pray and have inner peace."

"You could take the time to walk and meditate."

"Oh, do you remember when Alison and Henk and Holy Cow would cook stone soup on a camp fire in the middle of the labyrinth?"

"Stone soup?"

"Yeah, we put in carrots, frozen peas, a big pot of chicken stock. We would sing camp-fire songs until 10:00 p.m. when the guards came to tell Henk and Alison and Holy Cow it was time for them to go home! Alison would sing all night if she could!"

"And, remember that time someone—I can't remember who now—told the story of the two wolves?"

"That's such an awesome story."

"Tell me, I've never heard it!"

"Okay, it goes something like this: a Native American grandfather was talking to his grandson about how he felt. The grandfather said, "I feel as if I have two wolves fighting in my heart. One wolf is the vengeful, angry, violent one. The other wolf is the loving, compassionate one. The grandson asked him, "Which wolf will win the fight in your heart? The grandfather answered, 'The one I feed'."

"Remember Holy Cow teaching us that our life is a sacred journey?"

"Yeah there was a lot of talk about how ACCW was about change, growth, healing—"

"Changing our vision of what life can be like, discovery of who we are as women—"

"Courage and strength, love and respect for ourselves and others—"

"A transformation from the old to the new, love and inner peace."

The Labyrinth

LISA TORIKKA

IT ISN'T THE SAME as when we started but neither am I. The labyrinth at ACCW has changed over the years, but its intention remains the same: it is a place to feel safe, to meditate, to pray, to centre yourself, to think, or just a place to take a walk. You walk around until you come to the centre, to yourself. There you can think, meditate, or pray. Your soul and spirit are your guides.

I was a little anxious about starting to build a labyrinth with Alison. What was I getting myself into? When I pictured a labyrinth, I saw a hedged walkway of mazes; how were we to build this? But when she showed me pictures and Googled different labyrinths, I understood. They do not have to be perfect, and they do not have to have hedges. We can build one of rocks and sand. First, we blessed the ground with a fire that was built on our delegated spot from an Aboriginal Day celebration. Women wrote their hopes, fears, and prayers and offered them to that fire for Holy Cow to pray for guidance and closure, to heal their wounded spirits. Alison and I were the last to leave that sacred spot. I will never forget the peace I felt; it was the beginning of my healing journey. Within a week, we came up with a general idea of how we were to build our labyrinth. We had a starting point (which is different today than what it was then) and we began. We used grandfathers[1] from the sweat grounds and any other place we could pilfer them from. We trucked wheelbarrows upon wheelbarrows of sand. And we built. We made a path back and forth, around in a circle and then spiralled into the middle. Three to six women worked on it any given day, and some days, it was just me. Alison brought tiles, which we placed on the pathways, and it was beautiful. We patched the pond walls beside the labyrinth with cement. We put a big old grandfather in the middle of our cement patch, and wrote August 23, 2004. It was the official end date of the project, but the work will never be finished.

Over the years, our labyrinth has changed. Women have painted some of the grandfathers with inspirational words, taken the tiles out, put the tiles back in, let it over grow with weeds, weeded it, planted flowers in it, pulled flowers out. But one thing that has never changed, nor will ever change is the intention of our labyrinth.

In the years since the labyrinth was built, I have seen women walk it, talk about it, question it, and change it. During her incarceration, one woman prayed every morning, rain or shine, in our labyrinth. She really understood and that humbled me.

I learned many things from our labyrinth:

- If your intentions are good, you can do anything;
- If you have faith, your life will be filled with good things;
- Change is inevitable, but the choices you make along with change will make the difference;
- I believed that I could change—and I did. I believed that I could be happy—and I am. I believed that there is a better way, and oh, is there ever.

I owe a lifetime of gratitude to the people who passed those beliefs on to me, mostly Alison Granger-Brown. Without her wisdom, never giving up on me even when I gave up on myself, I would not be the woman I am today. Thank you, Alison.

---

[1]Grandfathers are rocks used in Aboriginal sweat traditions.

Flashback 6: Life in Prison
(Win2H meeting, November, 2010)

"My favourite memory is Alison's graduation."

"Yeah, that was awesome."

"She worked so hard on that degree! She'd go away every May for a month to go to school."

"How long did she do that?"

"For three years! Inmates and staff sometimes wondered how we would survive without her to run the prison activities. One day, after her last year away, we were having sports day and we arranged a fire drill right in the middle of it."

"I can't believe we could get the jail to put on a fake fire drill so we could get Alison to go to the middle of the field."

"I remember that! Alison was so mad! She kept saying, 'They shouldn't hold a fire drill during sports day!' 'How long is this going to take?'"

"She stormed to the upper meadow where everyone had gathered, waiting for her!"

"We made Alison a graduation cake, a graduation scroll, and a bright blue hat and gown, with a beautiful tassel!"

"How many times have any of us seen a graduation gown and cap? We had no idea what it looked like and we could not go on the Internet to find out. We went to the arts and crafts room and tried to imagine what it should look like."

"I still have it, it was like a top hat so tall!"

Hope Abecedarian[1]

Alison's office, Aboriginal Day, angel cards, acceptance

Barbeques, Baby Sierra, becoming healthy, belonging

Carnival, cotton candy, chalk drawings, connection, comfort, creativity

Drumming, dressing up, hip-hop dancing, dialogue in the research room

Eagle hut, Easter egg hunts, excited about making a difference, encouraging, energy

Forums for research, finding a voice, driving the forklift

Games, Alison's graduation, gym

Holy Cow, Halloween party, Happy Tuesday, hanging out with dogs, hope, heart

Ice cream, Ignition[2]

Joining in

Karaoke, working in the kitchen, kindness

Living with three babies, living on Alder, loving

Mattresses in the gym, mill outside the gates

Nail-painting

One-on-one talks

Puppet show, presents on the door, photos, parenting tips

Quiet

Running club, river, rocking chair, research team

Sweats, sports day, smoking, slip and slide, survey designing, safety, sharing, smiles

Tug (the dog)

Us

Volleyball, voice

Water fights, W2, wiener roasts, wanting to make a difference, warmth

Xmas parties

Yoga, dog yard

Zucchini in the vegetable garden

[1]This Abecedarian was created from a mapping exercise done by women participating in a writing workshop about the experiences and qualities that made ACCW a place of hope and renewal.
[2]Ignition is a music group that performed at the correctional centre.

Babies in Prison

Having my son at ACCW probably saved my life. He was my reason for getting out of bed every day. Alder was not like a unit at all, but like a home. Had I not been able to keep my son with me, I doubt that I would be doing everything that I am today. Everything I do, I'm doing so that I can make a better life for him.

—Teagen

Paragraphs of Passion

W

My passion is to get more parenting and baby programs.

X

My passions are deep and many. I look at our government and the ministry of children and families and wonder how they can remove children from their families to be put into homes. How many women change from that for the good? How many suffer and regress?

Y

My passion is adoption. I was adopted at seven days of age. I want to learn whether there is a link between being adopted and addiction and I want to delve into the emotional pain involved.

Z

I would like my kids to know a little about addiction so they understand that it wasn't their fault that I wasn't there for them.

A

I would like to learn more about crystal meth and how it affects a baby in the womb—the long term and short term side effects.

B

My passion is grief and how to deal with grief. There are powerful overwhelming emotions that on the outside we dealt with by using drugs and alcohol. How is one, when incarcerated, supposed to deal with loss? It is a huge issue if, not only deaths and losing a child, there is loss of many things that must be dealt with.

Doctor's Journey

RUTH ELWOOD MARTIN

THE WARDEN, BRENDA TOLE, phoned me today in clinic to ask, "As the prison physician, what is your opinion about the idea of women in prison, who deliver babies in hospital, being able to return here with their babies?" "What is my opinion?" I laughed, "This is the most sensible idea I've heard in years!" I thought about the endless milk-binding pills and anti-depressants that I have prescribed for incarcerated women who have returned to prison sans baby following their delivery. It has been heart wrenching to witness their grief, turning to guilt, despair, and hopelessness, and eventual deepening substance use in their quest for oblivion. "I will be delighted to be the prison baby family physician: newborn examinations, breast feeding coaching, newborn medical questions and whatever else is needed. Bring them on!"

—Journal entry

Incarcerated women are separated from their children for two reasons. Firstly, a woman's children may be apprehended by child welfare authorities sometime prior to incarceration because of maternal substance use; incarceration may intensify the emotional impact of a woman's separation from her children. Secondly, a woman's imprisonment may precipitate her geographic separation from her children.

Once imprisoned, a woman's physical separation from her children is exacerbated by the great distance of the female prison from her family and community, making children's visits and telephone calls financially difficult for families living in poverty. In Canada, from four percent (federal) to six percent (provincial) of the total incarcerated population is female (Kong and AuCoin 2008). There is one female institution in Canada for every nine, approximately, geographically dispersed male institutions (Correctional Service Canada).

An estimated 20,000 children each year are impacted by the incarceration of their mothers in Canada (Cunningham and Baker 4). Worldwide, an estimated six percent of incarcerated women are pregnant while serving prison time (Knight and Plugge 1). Providing prison mother-infant units to women who have given birth to their infants while incarcerated is considered normal practice in most countries in the world. Published reports of prison 'mother-infant units' exist for twenty-two countries including England, Wales, Australia, Brazil, Denmark, Finland, Germany, Greece, Italy, the Netherlands, New Zealand, Russia, Spain, Sweden, Switzerland, some U.S. states (ICPS), Kyrgyzstan, Ghana, Egypt, Mexico, India, Chile (Bedi; Institute of Women and Criminal Justice) and Thailand (Thailand Government). During the period 2005-2007, we were not aware of any infants residing with their mothers inside correctional institutions in Canada.

Babies should be exclusively breastfed until they are six months of age and then continue to be breastfed on demand until they are two years of age, according to international health experts, including the World Health Organization (WHO) and the American Academy of Paediatrics. Babies who are not breastfed may be at increased risk for diabetes, allergies, and gastrointestinal and respiratory infections (Health Canada 4; WHO). Breastfeeding is also important for psychosocial development—the associated physical contact, eye contact, and the quality of feeding promote attachment—in addition to the well-known health and nutritional benefits. The health disparities that breastfeeding can prevent are most prevalent among people living in poverty and among people of Aboriginal ancestry—groups that are over-represented in Canadian prison populations. However, establishing and maintaining breastfeeding on demand is not possible unless mothers and babies can be housed together with 24-hour contact.

In 2005, Brenda Tole initiated the Infant and Mother Health Initiative at the Alouette Correctional Centre for Women as a partnership between BC Corrections and the Ministry for Children and Family Development (MCFD), with the collaboration of BC Women's Hospital's Fir Square Combined Care Unit (BC Women's Hospital and Health Centre). Incarcerated women who gave birth, and who were deemed by MCFD able and willing to provide appropriate parental care, were able to keep their infants in their care while in prison. Thirteen babies were born to incarcerated mothers during the initiative's duration (2005-2007), nine of whom lived in prison with their mothers and stayed in prison until their mother's release. Eight babies were breastfed for the duration of their mother's prison stay. Fifteen months was the longest stay of any infant in prison.

In this chapter, we explore the health benefits of 'babies in prison' not only for the infants and mothers themselves, but for all incarcerated women and all prison staff.

REFERENCES

American Academy of Pediatrics. "Breastfeeding and the Use of Human Milk." *Pediatrics* 129 (3) (2012): 827-841.

Bedi, K. *It's Always Possible: Transforming One of the Largest Prisons in the World.* New Dehli: Stirling Paperbacks, 2006.

BC Women's Hospital and Health Centre. Briefing Note – Closure of ACCW Mother and Baby Program. 2008.

Correctional Service Canada. National Facility Directory. Web.

Cunningham, A. and L. Baker. *Waiting for Mummy: Giving a Voice to the Hidden Victims of Imprisonment.* London, ON: Centre for Children and Families in the Justice System, 2003.

Health Canada. "Duration of Exclusive Breastfeeding: Questions and Answers for Professionals—Infant Feeding." Government of Canada, 2004. Web.

International Centre for Prison Studies (ICPS). *International Profile of Women's Prisons.* London: ICPS, 2008.

Institute of Women and Criminal Justice. *Mothers, Infants and Imprisonment A National Look at Prison Nurseries and Community-Based Alternatives.* New York: Women's Prison Association, 2009.

Knight, M. and E. Plugge. "Risk Factors for Adverse Perinatal Outcomes in Imprisoned Pregnant Women: A Systematic Review." *BioMed Central Public Health* 5 (2005): 111. Web.

Kong, R. and K. AuCoin. "Female Offenders in Canada: Canadian Centre for Justice Statistics." *Statistics Canada* 28 (1) (2008): 1-16.

Thailand Government Public Relations Department. "Bangkok Rules." Adopted by the United Nations General Assembly. 2011. Web.

World Health Organization (WHO). "Nutrient Adequacy of Exclusive Breastfeeding for the Term Infant During the First Six Months of Life." Geneva: WHO, 2002.

When I was babysitting baby Jayden, I would be doing horticulture also. I would take Jayden with me to horticulture and I would be handing out the tools to the women in the morning and women would talk with Jayden. Jayden would bring up lots of emotions for women about their own children. For me, being away from my son, babysitting Jayden helped.
—Christine Hemingway

At night, I would lie in my room awake wondering what my own children looked like or where they were.
—Mo Korchinski

The prison, the staff, the inmates, and administration had all experienced the wonder of the babies.
—Kelly Murphy

Children at ACCW

BRENDA TOLE

IN 2003, I WAS ASSIGNED AS THE WARDEN of Alouette Correctional Centre for Women (ACCW) in Maple Ridge, BC. I oversaw the remodelling of an older facility that had housed provincial male offenders. ACCW, a medium security facility to house provincially sentenced women offenders opened in April 2004. Women centred programs and services had been developed for this new facility, and the staff (most of whom came from the previous provincial women's facility) received training developed specifically for women offenders.

While meeting with the key players around the health-care component for the new facility, the director of a maternity unit at BC Women's Hospital requested that we consider the possibility of babies who were born to mothers in custody returning with their mothers to the correctional centre in order to facilitate breast-feeding and nurturing.

With the support of Corrections Branch Headquarters, the ACCW Healthcare team, correctional staff (both managers and line staff) and other provincial ministry personnel, it was decided we could facilitate the return of mothers and babies to ACCW when recommended by the hospital and agreed to by the Ministry of Children and Family (MCFD) who had final authority over the placement of the child. The decisions to place the mother and child together at the correctional facility were made by an interdisciplinary team consisting of the key staff from Vancouver Women's Hospital, ACCW healthcare, ACCW administration, MCFD and first nations bands if the woman was first nations. The mother and her family were included in all the stages of this process.

When mothers returned to the correctional facility with their babies, the babies stayed at the facility until their mothers were discharged. The longest stay was fifteen months. The babies' health and development was monitored by the Ministry of Health community nurses, ACCW healthcare, and MCFD social workers. Release planning for the majority of the mothers and babies included placement at a residential supportive residence that took mothers and their young infants. The residential placement helped the women make the transition to the community with support from the staff there.

Being involved in the initiative with Women's Hospital had a profound effect on me personally, on the women directly involved, the staff and other women offenders, and the ministries and community agencies who partnered with us.

From a personal perspective I was struck by how, initially, other agencies and ministries were surprised and cautious regarding the proposal of the newborn babies returning to the facility with their mothers. It took time and many discussions and meetings for all the players to feel comfortable to work with Women's Hospital and us on this initiative. I was also struck by a general feeling that, for many people, the rights of the child to be with the mother for bonding and breastfeeding was overshadowed by the feeling that this privilege should not be afforded to the incarcerated mothers. Although it is accepted around the world that nursing infants and/or small children remain with their mothers when incarcerated, this is rarely seen in Canada. As the initiative continued and more mothers came back to the facility with their babies, I could personally see the attitudes of many shift from cautious and guarded to comfortable and supportive. I found the community agencies were quite willing to provide supportive services to the children and mothers within the facility reducing the need to develop programs and services specific to this special population.

The mothers involved expressed great joy and were grateful that they could continue to breastfeed and nurture their babies at the facility. They participated in all that was asked of them to ensure the safety and health of their babies. Other women at the facility had to deal with the reminder of the pain they suffered from being away from their children while incarcerated. Seeing the babies triggered feelings of loss, but a general feeling of hope permeated the entire population and the atmosphere at the facility was more positive in many ways.

Seeing other ministries and agencies support this initiative impacted many of the women. Most had very little trust in government agencies due to negative interactions in their past. Seeing the agencies working together to have the babies stay with their mothers gave them a different perspective from which to view these groups. Some voiced a new interest to work with agencies to initiate contact with children they had lost contact with or to work to improve their own lives to make a better life for their children.

Seeing the mothers and babies thrive at the facility and be released to the community together continued to reinforce the feeling that this initiative was not only the child's right, but also the right thing to do for the child.

With the presence of babies, the prison as a whole was different. There was less violence, less bullying and swearing. The environment in the prison was less intimidating and more welcoming for first time offenders. I had been incarcerated back in 2005 when the first mother and child arrived at ACCW. Now two years later, several mothers and their children have gone through the program.

—Kelly Murphy

Tanya's Story

TANYA NEWELL

WHEN I ARRIVED AT ACCW with a twenty-month sentence, I was two months pregnant. Facing the possibility of losing my child, the months ahead filled me with stress and emotional instability. I inquired about the possibility of keeping my baby with me in prison and I learned that our warden, Brenda Tole, was a very open-minded woman willing to try new things. Dr. Martin, the prison doctor, suggested I write a letter to the Directors and she gave me her support.

At the end of July, I was granted an Unescorted Temporary Absence to attend a four- to six-week program at BC Women's Hospital where I completed courses in parenting, alcohol and drugs, relationship counselling, methadone withdrawal, acupuncture therapy, and infant respiratory management.

While I was at BC Women's Hospital, Brenda Tole and other prison officials met the Director of Health Care and a social worker with the Ministry of Children and Family Development. They agreed to assist me to remain with my son because the bond between mother and son is especially beneficial. They decided to start the Infant and Mother Health Initiative at ACCW in order to support both my son and me in prison. I was also supported by the other women and staff. I believe the Infant and Mother Health Initiative in Prison will assist many women who are incarcerated to gain the will and motivation needed to go home to their own kids, rather than returning to their old behaviour which led them into the prison system in the first place.

It was a slap in the face that ended up being really healing for me. We are really good at denying our emotions. I was in ACCW when the first baby was there, Tanya's baby, and I remember feeling really angry and jealous. I told myself I wasn't going anywhere near that baby. Then, when I came back in 2007, there were two babies and one pregnant woman. Something changed for me. I requested to live in the unit with the babies and the pregnant women. I can't say what was going on inside me, I just wanted to be on that unit, and that was what healed me. I did a lot of work on myself; I would look at those children and face my own shame and guilt. The constant exposure to those kids and their softness was healing for me.

—Kelly Murphy

Kelly's Story

GUILT AND SHAME saturates incarcerated women. Their lives of crime and substance misuse have been arrested. As they are forced to withdraw from their source of numbness, the consequences of their actions begin to reveal themselves. The majority of us are mothers, mothers who have distanced themselves from their children. This separation, the perpetual feelings of guilt, and the despair of not being able to mend relationships blinded my vision of hope.

I was incarcerated at Alouette Correctional Centre for Women and lived in the mother and baby unit. At the time, I didn't realize that being subjected to the mothers and their children would be a catalyst for one of the most profound transformations in my life. These pregnant women, newborns, and even a little toddler, became my teachers.

Yet, when I first arrived on the mother and baby unit, the babies were crying and toys were strewn in what appeared to be a daycare; I was second-guessing my decision to move onto the "quiet unit." As with any unit change within the prison setting, one has to undergo the scrutiny of unit residents who decide whether you will fit in. Even though I was welcomed, I vowed that I wasn't going to get close to the mothers and definitely not to their children. I witnessed my own bitterness at my broken relationship with my daughter.

So, what was I going to do with this bitterness? I understood that it was a wound that kept me clouded in an opiate haze and that kept me re-offending in order to maintain the euphoria. The problem was, as the years moved forward, the pain intensified, the drugs stopped working, and my daughter was becoming more damaged by the abandonment of her mother. It was time to get a grip, pull myself out of selfishness, and mend the hurt between my daughter and me. I saw the babies as an opportunity to confront my failures as a mother and to open my heart into loving. I had a desire to change.

114

Six months of living on the mother and baby unit was healing. There were tears, laughter, conflicts, pain, all of it therapeutic. I never would have thought that these little babies would provide the strength and motivation that I needed to make a change. To not return to the life that was familiar, but to return to a life that was unfamiliar, a life with responsibility as a mother, a daughter, and a friend.

Mo's Story

MO KORCHINSKI

THE BIG TURNAROUND FOR ME was when the jail started a program for mothers and babies. A friend of mine delivered and brought a son back to prison to live with her until her sentence was up. For the longest time, when anyone asked me if I had children, I would say no. It was easier than explaining where my children were.

But seeing my friend with her baby woke something inside me and I started to yearn for my children. I had no idea where my children were or what they looked like or even if they were alive. That's a horrible place to be—in jail, feeling like the worst mother in the world. I was in jail for eight months, and out for eight weeks, then back in for 15 months. This time, other women had their babies with them and the feelings of wanting to be a mother grew with every day that I saw these women with their babies.

There were now three babies inside the prison, and I decided to ask for help. I don't like asking for help. I don't want to owe people or feel in debt, but I wanted to find my children. A welfare and youth counsellor made some calls for me. I found out that my oldest daughter was not in the system anymore and her file was closed—a dead end. I phoned 411 for the children's fathers' phone numbers, but no go there. I lost hope that I would be able to find them, and I didn't know how to deal with these feelings.

When I was high for all those years, I learned to live in denial. I tried to forget that I had children. In prison, clean and sober and seeing babies all around slapped me in the face. But at the same time, it was a start for me to heal and deal with my issues as a person, as a mother. It brought up a lot of feelings that I'd kept buried for a long time regarding my own children and my own childhood. At times, it was so overwhelming that I didn't know what to do with the feelings.

Yearning

MO KORCHINSKI

the swell of her belly
rippling from within
new life grows
waits to be free
just like me
locked up in jail
watching babies play
laugh and cry
while mothers glow
with God's best gift
yearning wondering
where are mine?
what do they look like?
are they alive?
hoping praying
this will be
my last time
doing time

Participatory Health Research

Dr. Martin wants us to get high on doing research!
      —Member of prison participatory research team

Paragraphs of Passion

C

All I can offer the research team is my honest and serious hard work and strive to help other women like me.

D

I am willing to do whatever is necessary to be a positive influence to this team. I am experienced in all aspects of writing, typing, and computer work. I look forward to working and being a part of this team.

E

I enjoy transcribing. Since being on the research team, I have learned a lot about computers and am thankful for that. My passion would be to continue to do transcribing.

F

I'm going to research single parenting: young, old, fathers, and mothers. How many get their children taken? What does it feel like to a single parent? I'm going to interview my mom, my daughter, and my father.

G

I've been using crystal meth for almost ten years and although I personally have not experienced a great deal of physical or mental damage, I am aware of, and have seen, the damaging effects it has had on my friends and associates. It is my hope that my research project will help inform those like myself to be educated of the impending danger should they continue down the path they have been on.

H

An area I am interested in learning more about is anorexia and bulimia.

I am anorexic in the way I abuse my body by not eating for days if I am even a little upset. That is something I really want to change and maybe learning more about it will help me with that.

I
I am interested in researching teenage addiction and how little housing and support there is for them.

Doctor's Journey

RUTH ELWOOD MARTIN

IN THE SPRING OF 2005, while I was studying an on-line Action Research course, I had an "Aha!" moment—a light bulb experience. What would happen if women in prison could research their own health issues? What would a collaborative research project, a project grounded in the women's lived experience, tell us about their health concerns? I realized that this was the type of research we should be doing in prison.
—Journal entry

After I had seen several women inside prison with cases of invasive cervical cancer, I knew that I should do something to answer the research question, 'How can we improve cervical cancer screening for women in prison?' This questioning led us to design, implement, and evaluate a prison cervical cancer screening intervention pilot project (Martin; Martin et al. 2004, 2008). It was a small step forward toward improving the health of women in prison, although increasing the number of Pap smears in prison did not seem the most pressing health priority for most of the women inside prison.

In 2005, I realized that participatory health research was the type of research to do inside a women's prison: ask the women themselves what they would like to research in order to improve their health— what their research questions are—and, then, invite them to be partners in designing the research methods, gathering the data, analyzing, and interpreting the data.

Constellations of events coincided to develop this research notion further: a chance bathroom conversation with Vivian Ramsden, a family medicine researcher experienced in participatory health research, who agreed to mentor me; an enthusiastic conversation with Alison Granger-Brown, prison recreation therapist, at the prison gates as we were leaving work; and, the support of Brenda Tole, prison warden, who viewed a proposed prison participatory health research project as congruent with her overall philosophy of prison as a therapeutic community.

I assumed that we needed some funding to conduct participatory research inside prison, so we applied for a small development research grant from the Canadian Institute of Health Research (CIHR), which was to develop an application for an operating grant for participatory research inside prison. However, the dilemma when applying for a research grant for participatory research is that you don't know what you are researching because the "research subjects" should be engaged in decisions regarding study questions and study methods! As a first step, we decided to hire a summer student to interview incarcerated women and prison guards with, "If we were to conduct participatory research inside this prison, what would it look like?" and, "If you were asked to design research to improve the health of women in prison, what health issues would you focus on?"

We poured over the transcripts of these interviews and discussions, and gleaned numerous themes, ideas and suggestions that incarcerated women and the prison guards had suggested as ways to improve health. It was overwhelming—the list seemed endless. No "saturation of data" in sight!

Vivian Ramsden, mentoring this process from Saskatchewan, suggested that the entire prison community should come together for a research forum, to discuss the summer interview findings and to discuss ways forward for our prison participatory research funding application to CIHR. She gently reminded me that, after all, in a participatory research grant application all of the research "subjects" should participate in generating the study design. I groaned at the amount of work and chaos that this would entail: firstly, I needed to ask Brenda Tole, the warden, if a whole prison research forum would be feasible; secondly, we would need to pull the forum together, like organizing a wedding; thirdly, the deadline for the CIHR grant application was looming (November 1, 2005), with an enormous amount of work to complete before then.

Brenda Tole and the management team of ACCW were supportive of the proposal, and they decided on a date for the forum: it was to be a day-long meeting, in the prison gym, for all incarcerated women and prison staff, management, and contractors. Four academic colleagues attended from University of British Columbia, and Vivian Ramsden flew in from the prairies, arriving on the morning of the forum. Viv and I planned the forum agenda together as we drove the thirty miles from Vancouver airport to ACCW, and as I asked her, "You are the expert here—what are we going to do today?" Vivian's advice to me, then, as always, was, "Trust the process."

A storm blew through that morning and felled a tree onto the power lines. When we arrived at ACCW, the emergency generator was whirring and the prison gym was lit with reduced lighting. Women were crowded into the gym, sitting on fitness mats and chairs around the periphery. Altogether, 120 incarcerated women, ten correctional centre staff (correctional management and officers; contracted health and inter-professional staff), and five academic researchers attended the forum. Aboriginal Elder Holy Cow invited us to begin the ceremonies by holding hands in a large circle around the gym—inmates, guards, academics, and contractors. She stood in the centre, with the prison Chaplain beside her, and said a prayer in Cree, translated into English, followed by a prayer spoken by the Chaplain. This opening ceremony served to bring "spirituality" into the health research agenda of the day's events and, indeed, into the health research agenda over the ensuing years.

The prison research forum that day was a pivotal event. If the research forum had not occurred, there would have been no future participatory research project; conversely, all the participatory research events that followed emerged because of that first forum. I still get goose bumps when I remember that day. I tell my friends and colleagues that, short of birthing my children and getting married, that day was the most significant of my life.

I explained to the gathered audience the reason for our gathering. Vivian Ramsden shared some stories of transformation written by men and women of the inner city of Saskatoon who had engaged in participatory health research. I shared the themes that had emerged from the summer student project and invited comments and thoughts from the audience. With Holy Cow assigning the microphone to participants as if the mic was a talking stick, women one-by-one came to share their thoughts and ideas, their suggestions and yearnings about how to improve health. The women listened to each other speak. They applauded and laughed and cried. The guards also came to the microphone and shared their ideas, as did the academics.

As we talked, Vivian Ramsden wrote on a flip chart the values that were being expressed: 1) Respect; 2) Break the silence; 3) Listen and be heard; 4) Building on assets (strengths) rather than deficits; 5) All who wish to be involved in the research process may be involved. Everyone present in the gym—incarcerated women, guards, academics, contractors—agreed that these five values were essential and integral to any research project moving forward.

By the end of the afternoon, we gathered into five smaller discussion groups. Each group focused on one theme, and brainstormed ideas for interventions. Women and guards could select which discussion group to join. Most women chose to join the groups that focused on "life skills and re-entry into society" and "children, family, and relationships." Fewer women joined the groups about "mental health and addictions" and "HIV, hepatitis, and infections." This was the first of many future times that I would learn to listen to the process of women identifying their priorities for their health.

The next morning, Saturday, Vivian Ramsden and I invited all women who wanted to assist with writing the funding application to join us. Saturday morning, there were twenty-seven incarcerated women present in the gym ready and willing to assist! They offered to type up the audio-recordings of the forum, working in threes, not having transcription gear: one would read aloud the audio, another would write the words long-hand, while a third woman typed. Other women offered to gather letters of support, "Like impact statements—we know how to write those." They offered to scribe dictated letters for women who did not know how to write. The women asked the warden (who agreed) if "research team work" could become their prison work placement, in lieu of other prison work, such as laundry or unit maintenance. We had two weeks to pull the funding application together, and we did it, together.

REFERENCES

Martin, R. Elwood "Would Female Inmates Accept Papanicolaou Smear Screening if It Was Offered to Them During their Incarceration?" *Canadian Journal of Public Health/Revue canadienne de santé publique* 162 (5) (2000): 657-658.

Martin, R. Elwood, T. G. Hislop, G. D. Grams, B. Calam, E. Jones, and V. Moravan. "Evaluation of a Cervical Cancer Screening Intervention for Prison Inmates." *Canadian Journal of Public Health/Revue canadienne de santé publique* 95 (4) (2004): 285-289.

Martin, R. Elwood, T. G. Hislop, V. Moravan, G. D. Grams, and B. Calam. "Three-year Follow-up Study of Women Who Participated in a Cervical Cancer Screening Intervention While in Prison." *Canadian Journal of Public Health/Revue canadienne de santé publique* 99 (4) (2008): 262-266.

Staff began to see women differently. Their attitude changed. With the research presentations, the dialogue, what women had accomplished, wanting to be more involved. Initially the staff were not that engaged. Then they were impressed by the women's energy, by their interest, by the changes, their dedication—people responded to that. Everybody came out of the research forums learning.

—Brenda Tole, Warden

First Forum

KELLY MURPHY

IT'S DIFFICULT TO PUT INTO WORDS what it felt like to be in that first forum in October of 2005. It was very odd to see over 100 inmates and the Corrections staff, as well as community members from outside the prison, gathered together in the auditorium. I don't think many of us inmates knew what was actually going on, but we had heard there would be snacks from the "outside" and pizza for lunch, so we quickly rushed to find our seats. We were told that we had the ability to implement change in the health of incarcerated women; now and in the future. I was awestruck as Dr. Martin and her colleagues addressed the room full of broken women about how we could come together as women and work on ways to get our lives back. The closest I can get to describing it is "magical," thrilling and now in hindsight, miraculous.

We broke into smaller groups so that we could brainstorm the different topics that had been brought to the table. As ideas began to percolate, women were given the microphone so that they could share their ideas. Women who had always been quiet boldly stepped up to the microphone to voice their opinions and suggestions. My heart began to swell as these women, insignificant to the outside world, found their voice, found themselves. There is nothing more gratifying to me than the look of hope in a woman's eyes.

I don't think there were many women sleeping that night in the camp; we were pumped up on empowerment, many of us anticipating the meeting called for the following day for those who wanted to participate in the research project inside the prison gates. I was excited about the possibilities; if I got on board, I knew I could make a difference. And, if I got involved with the research project, well, I knew the work would influence me in a way where I might actually make changes in my own life. But I wasn't ready for the commitment. Weeks later I was released and I returned to what was familiar: crime and addiction.

Reflections on My Days at ACCW

VIVIAN RAMSDEN

I am always awed by how life unfolds. Several months earlier, Ruth and I had spoken of undertaking face-to-face meetings with the women at ACCW and members of the research team. When I received an outline and invitation to the face-to-face meeting, I made plane reservations to go to Vancouver, not knowing all of the various elements, locations, times, etc. Ruth was away on a much needed holiday in Spain. As I embarked on this adventure, I knew that since we had agreed upon the date, things would unfold as it should. The flights I had chosen and the time of arrival were perfect. Ruth kindly picked me up at the airport. As we drove to ACCW, we had an opportunity to talk about how the day before us might evolve.

I have had the opportunity to use and be engaged in facilitating participatory methods while working within a framework of community action for a number of years in rural and remote settings, urban under-served settings, First Nations settings, and international settings. I am always awed by the fact that at the first encounter neither the individuals/clients/patients/inmates nor the health-care practitioners/staff realize the expertise that each is bringing to the encounter. Each group seems to know and understand its own position within the world in which they live and work but rarely, if ever, share their knowledge and understandings with the other. Transformative learning aims to address this lack of communication and collaboration. Transformative learning refers to the process by which we re-construct our ways of knowing to make them more inclusive; participate in value-based critical thinking; and take appropriate actions based on the resulting insights (Mezirow, J. and Associates). I have learned over the years that stories integrated into the world of science add significance to the individuals, the relationships and the organizations/ systems. I have also learned that trusting people to solve problems generates higher levels of motivation and better solutions.

On the drive to ACCW, I asked Ruth if an Elder would be present because it would be important for the Elder to open with a prayer. The answer was uncertain; however, when we arrived at ACCW (after ducking under a power line downed by a tree that had cracked and fallen on the power line and shut off the power at ACCW), the Elder named Holy Cow and the Chaplain were already in attendance.

As the women and staff arrived at the gymnasium, there was an air of anticipation mingled with an air of wonder. The Elder and the Chaplain shared in the tradition of opening with a prayer, which built the spiritual dimension into the plan for the day. It also seemed to set the tone for engaging the community in process. Ruth talked about the process and why the women were invited to participate in this research endeavour. I shared stories from individuals residing in the underserved areas of Saskatoon who had engaged in participatory methods integrated with action research. The women were then invited to speak and the microphone was used as a talking stick so that the individual with the microphone was able to freely share with the whole group, which consisted of the women, the guards/staff, and members of the research team, including the warden.

The women initially focused on their personal challenges, but this soon gave way to sharing stories about how the staff at ACCW works with them to achieve the best possible outcomes. A significant breakthrough had been made when one of the women delivered a baby and the baby had been able to remain with the mother during her incarceration, which marked the beginning of the prison mother and baby program. This baby brings sunshine to a world that contains a lot of darkness. Several women had gone through the system a number of times over a number of years. They were both formal and informal leaders and these early adopters engaged in trying out these new ideas (Rogers), which helped to establish a positive environment to undertake this research collaboration.

I felt very honoured to be a part of this historic event. Because of my familiarity with participatory methods, utilization of facilitation, and my belief that trusting people to solve problems generates higher levels of motivation and better solutions, sometimes it is hard to see just how much of a historic event it really was and/or is. I believe that the women, staff, and research team were working toward a common goal: to enhance the health and well-being of women during incarceration at ACCW. There was an overall sense of hope. Several projects that were deemed very important by the women were also deemed to be very important by the staff and the research team such as an orientation program for ACCW. This would be very easy to do—the women could conjointly develop the program with the staff and health-care practitioners, implement and subsequently evaluate the program—thus, building skills that could be utilized both at ACCW and in the communities to which the women return. In addition, the transmission of diseases would be mitigated; a win/win for everyone and it would build success in a way that talking about such an endeavour is unable to do.

The women brought knowledge and time to the work; the staff and health-care practitioners brought knowledge and skills to the work; the members of the research team brought knowledge and skills in evaluation/research to the work; the Elder and the Chaplain brought spirit to the work; and the participatory methods brought gifts of empowerment and worthiness to the work. The body, mind, and spirit were engaged in the process of building community with and by community, which resulted in enhanced health and well-being of all engaged in the process.

Ruth and I were the only members of the research team returning to ACCW on Saturday morning and we were unsure about the number of women and staff who would return and continue the dialogue. I had the opportunity to facilitate capturing the voices of the women on computer as they discussed the various elements—this was done in a transparent way with the use of an LCD Projector so that the women were also engaging in ensuring that the perceptions that I had understood and entered were accurate. All of the women present participated in some way and agreed to further participate in typing up the transcripts, entering the data collected in the small groups from the previous day, and engaging in the writing process the following week. As we packed up to go, everyone seemed to be enthusiastic and thoughtful about next steps and the women were allowed to use the time that they spent on this project as "work time" for which they received remuneration.

From previous experience, I found that the strength of the process helped me to understand that when we learned together we had an opportunity to celebrate the successes together. Having each woman share her story was very powerful and it broke down the barriers between the individuals/inmates, staff, health-care practitioners, and the research team, thus, resulting in a partnership. I am humbled by processes like these in which we learn together the realities of the worlds in which we live and work. I am honoured to have been invited to be a part of this process and to work with the women, staff, health-care practitioners, and members of the research team.

As this is a journey, the end or outcomes are yet unknown but regardless of these, the process will build relationships and empower women, staff, health-care practitioners, and the systems. This participatory research project has the potential to impress upon the Canadian Institutes of Health Research (CIHR) the importance of having members of the various communities as collaborators because the result will not only be better but will be building from the realities of the community rather than those external to it. In addition, the women, staff, research team and the system will learn different things from each other and different ways of engaging in research that will be sustainable long after the project has been completed.

REFERENCES

Mezirow, J. & Associates. *Fostering Critical Reflection in Adulthood: A Guide to Transformative and Emancipatory Learning.* San Francisco: Jossey-Bass Publishers, 2008.

Roger, E. *Diffusion of Innovations.* 5th ed. New York: Simon and Schuster, 2003.

The Research Office

RUTH ELWOOD MARTIN

AFTER WE HAD SUBMITTED the grant application, I anticipated an eight-month hiatus while we waited for the funding committee's review decision. However, the women in prison explained to me, "We don't need funding. We have lots of time on our hands and we want to learn." The women offered to do the research themselves. This work was too important to them. They successfully petitioned the warden to let "research team work" become a permanent work placement position inside the prison. Up to fifteen women met daily on the prison participatory health research team—some women stayed on the team for one or two weeks, others for several months—and, over the next twenty-two months, almost 200 women became members of the research team.

We had no research staff, because of the lack of funding, with the resultant serendipity that the incarcerated women guided every aspect of the research process. Several academic members on the team visited the prison to provide research skill-building workshops for the women. For myself, I decided to shift between two roles: I would "do research" with the women in the prison research room on Mondays as "Dr Ruth the researcher"; and, I would "do medicine" in the prison clinic on Tuesdays as "Dr Martin the doctor." The women seemed to accept this.

The research days became a bit like "kitchen table wisdom" (Remen) over cups of tea, as the women talked about what they were interested in—whatever topic they were researching at the time. It felt a more meaningful use of my time. I began to enjoy my days in the research room more than my days in the clinic. At times I felt like a mother, at times like a mentor, at times a big sister, at times a research expert, at times a translator or educator of medical information. But, most times, I felt like the learner.

Incarcerated women peer researchers developed an orientation package that they invited new members joining the research team to complete. The orientation package included: a "welcome to the women's health research team"' work-placement questionnaire including questions about a member's computer skills and skills they wished to acquire; a "new member questionnaire" including a demographic self-survey and health-related questions; a drug of choice paragraph and survey which asked peer researchers to describe their illicit drug use; an optional life story exercise in which women were invited to write about meaningful life events; and finally, a peer researcher confidentiality agreement and consent form.

The women developed a "paragraph of passion" exercise, which asked new members of the research team to write a response to the question: "What area do you want to learn more about in order to improve your health and the health of others?" I marvelled as I witnessed this process, because women in prison were following their own passions to research. It could be anything, including homelessness, drugs, foster care, health care inside and outside of prison, nutrition, dentists, culture, job skills, schooling and training, community support, and exercise.

The prison peer research team also developed a daily routine for themselves that included 'angel words' (each person in turn randomly selected an angel card from a closed bag and shared with the group what their word meant to them that day) and a reading from a spiritual reflection book. These routines often led to discussions, related to their spiritual and emotional healing, which fostered an atmosphere of peer support within the research team. My favourite part of the day was joining in the angel cards routine, because this exercise seemed to root us together in something bigger than what we might accomplish on our own. And, I was often moved to awe, humbled, as I listened to their spiritual journeys, and as I appreciated the depth of their understanding and their resilience.

In addition, the prison peer research team developed organizational processes that provided opportunities for them to develop leadership within the group (e.g. administrative and organizational skills, public speaking, liaising with correctional staff, and peer mentoring in computer, language, and writing skills). They also invited academic researchers for participatory qualitative analysis workshops, writing workshops, and research discussions. They designed a webpage to communicate project findings and community resource information for women leaving prison.

The strong representation of Aboriginal women in the prison research team influenced the peer research team processes, and they included Aboriginal methods of dialogue and models of holistic health and healing. For example, the peer research team often discussed topics in a talking circle, practising a circular and equitable method of discussion. An object that represented a talking stick was often passed around the circle inviting everyone in turn to add their voice to the discussion without interruption.

The women of the prison participatory research team decided to organize and host prison health and education research forums, approximately monthly, modelled on the initial forum of October 2005. During these forums, women presented on health and education topics, which they themselves had been researching; they invited all women and staff of the prison to attend and participate in the resultant discussions, as well as members of community organizations, funding organizations, policy makers, government agencies and academic researchers. As a result of the forums, the prison research team compiled an extensive library of PowerPoint health education presentations that they had created on an array of health and education topics of their choice. (See list of topics, page 118).

In addition, the women of the prison research team were invited to talk to the local high school about the harmful effects of drug and alcohol use. In preparation for the talk, they chose street clothes from the prison thrift store. They also picked out jeans for me and Alison, so that the teenagers might not be able to distinguish the recreation therapist and prison physician from the women on the research team! When nine women walked out in single file onto the high school stage, in a line, to the music of the Red Hot Chili Peppers, and the applause of about 150 Grade 11 students, I felt as if my heart would burst.

The women on the prison research team read books about, "how to do survey research," and they wrote and conducted cross-sectional surveys of their peers (after obtaining UBC Research Ethics Certificates) about topics that *they* felt were relevant for their health, such as housing, smoking, exercise and nutrition, and their relationships with their children and families.

Through these prison research processes, nine health goals emerged; they grew out of the five health categories that had been identified during the forum. We conceptualized the nine health goals as a "bubble diagram," and posted a draft on the wall of the prison dining room to invite everyone's feedback. The nine health goals reflect incarcerated women's desire for health not only inside prison, but also in the community after their release from prison, and are:

- Improved relationships with children, families and partners;
- Improved peer and community support;
- Increased access to safe and stable housing;
- Improved access to individualized health care;
- Increased job skills, relevant education and employment;
- Improved dentition and oral health;
- Improved health awareness and integration (spiritual, emotional, mental, physical) including exercise and nutrition;
- Improved health and disease knowledge;
- Increased ability to contribute to society.
  (Martin et al., 2009)

By listening to the women in prison, the academic researchers and I were able to let go of our preconceived notions of the key objectives of this health research project, with our focus on research of diseases such as HIV addiction, and hepatitis C.

I realized that participatory health research embraces many disciplines, including education, and many ways of knowing, including many ways of asking questions in order to make sense of disease. I came to learn that incarcerated women's views of health and healing incorporates physical, emotional, mental, and spiritual health and healing. I also came to learn to trust health research processes that are built on values, such as the five values agreed upon during the first forum. And, overall, I witnessed women in prison as they moved along their health journey, educating not only themselves, but also each other, the warden, prison staff, health-care staff, and academics. They were taking responsibility for their own health and their own education, and that of their peers and their community, thereby breaking down stereotypes, misconceptions, and barriers.

REFERENCES

Martin, R. E., K. Murphy, D. Hanson, C. Hemingway, V. Ramsden, J. Buxton, A. Granger-Brown, L. L. Condello, M. Buchanan, N. Espinoza-Magana, G. Edworthy, and T. G. Hislop. "The Development of Participatory Health Research Among Incarcerated Women in a Canadian Prison." *International Journal of Prisoner Health* 5 (2) (2009): 95-107.
Remen, R. N. *Kitchen Table Wisdom: Stories that Heal.* New York: Riverhead Trade, 1997.

I'm proud of what the women accomplished—doing that work [developing and presenting the PowerPoints and developing the surveys] reminded us women why we were in prison— the research projects were the heart of the transformation that happened in the prison—every project changed peoples' lives, both the women who were listening and attending the research forums, the women who participated in the surveys, and especially the women who did the research on their own passion, who developed the PowerPoints/surveys and who presented on that topic.

—Mo Korchinksi

PowerPoint Presentations that Women Created and Presented

Changes of Incarcerated Women • Parole from Canadian Incarceration • History of Residential School • HIV & Your Immune System • Learning to Love Yourself • Participatory Research • Al-Anon and Alateen • Parenting Teenagers • Aboriginal Research • A Life of Addiction • Bulimia Nervosa • Babies in Prison • Smoking in Jail • Co-dependency • Crystal Meth • Proper Diets • Methadone • Diabetes • Exercise • Cocaine • Parole • Grief • SARS • Persons with Permanent Disabilities • Prison Mothers and Children • Housing and Homelessness • 1st and 2nd Stage Housing • Grandmother Hypothesis • Horticulture at ACCW • Fitness and Nutrition • Anxiety and Phobias • Native Spirituality • Man and Violence • Bi-Polar Disorder • Hepatitis A, B, C • Self-Mutilation • Life Stories • Alcoholism • Shoplifting • Addiction • Cannabis • Doulas • Heroin • Cardio • Lupus • HIV

[1]This list is of all the topics that the women on the participatory research team researched and developed PowerPoint presentations. The topics grew from their paragraphs of passion.

Surveys Created by Women on the Research Team

Homeless and Housing Survey
Has finding housing or not having a place to go to when you get out of jail been a problem for you before?
Did you get information about finding housing in the community before you left?

Shop Lifting
Do you have a problem with shoplifting?
Do you shoplift even when you have money?
Do you feel the urge to take something most times you are in a store?

Smoking
What are some of the positive benefits you get from smoking?
What are some of the reasons you want to change your smoking habits?

Sleep Issues
Do you have trouble sleeping at night?
Are you on sleeping medication?
Does the guard's flashlight wake you up at night?

Dental Survey
Are you in need of dental care?
Do you need to see a dentist?
Is financial hardship the reason for you not having your dental work done?

Appropriate Behaviour
What kind of physical contact do you think is okay in jail?
Do you believe in healthy boundaries in all settings?

Child Apprehension Survey
Are your children in the Ministry of Children and Family Development's care? Are you allowed visitation?

Physical Fitness and Nutrition
What type of physical fitness do you participate in?
Is physical fitness important to you?

MRSA Super Bug
Do you know what MRSA is?
Have you ever heard about MRSA skin infection?

Health Status Survey
Have you ever struggled with addiction?
Are you currently in contact with your family or friends?
Do you know your family medical history?

Inmate Survey
Would you like healthier choices offered on canteen?
Would you be interested taking any correspondence courses?
Do you feel comfortable talking about your needs to the guards or other resource staff?

Computer Use
Do you feel comfortable using a computer?
If no, would a list of step by step instructions help you feel more comfortable using a computer?

Weekly Skills Acquisition
How would you rate your health knowledge PRIOR to joining the ACCW research team?
How would you rate your health knowledge today?

Prison Mothers and Their Children
If you have more than one child, were/are they separated from each other?
How long have you been separated from your children?
Do/did you see your children and/or have visits with your children?

Art Therapy Evaluation
How helpful do you find art therapy in dealing with negative emotions inside prison?
How useful do you find art therapy in dealing with memories of past trauma?

Orientation Package for New Research Team Members
What is your passion? What would you like to research to help to improve the health of women in prison?

Please share with us your age, your level of education, your sentence level, your ethnicity and other demographics.

What is your drug of choice? Please write and share your story with us.
What is your life story? Please write and share your story with us.

"Doing Research" Inside Prison

KELLY MURPHY

IT WAS INEVITABLE that I would return to ACCW and when I did the research team was going strong. In fact, it had become an in-prison job placement. I signed up. Every day close to fifteen inmates would meet in the multi-purpose room to "do research." In the mornings, we checked in, shared our feelings, and shared our thoughts on the daily "angel word." The afternoons were spent researching various afflictions that had compromised our health and the effects of the different substances that kept us imprisoned. Once a month, a topic was presented at a community forum that was attended by inmates, prison staff, and community members. Many women were transformed as they wrote their life stories and paragraphs of passion. There were many tears, a lot of laughter, and women supporting each other with love as we wrote, some of us for the first time, about hopes, dreams, loss, and grief.

The passion I first felt as part of that first forum burns on inside me. I am blessed to have the opportunity to still "do research" and to support other women as they leave prison. Here we are on the "outside," Women in2 Healing working together to keep that dream alive. The dream that women once incarcerated, victims of our circumstances, could actually break free from the revolving door to find good health and ourselves.

Flashback 7: Participatory Health Research in Prison
(Win2H meeting, November, 2010)

"The research group got together in the mornings and we shared angel words. Each one of us got a word and said what it means to us."

"When we started to do the research with Dr. Martin, there was a huge shift in the way the guards viewed women in prison."

"The research program became a job placement with up to 15 women working on researching their own passion."

"We learned a variety of skills from working on the research team—"

"Working as a team player—"

"Data collecting, computer skills—"

"Making power point presentations, public speaking—"

"And survey skills!"

"Remember how we'd put on those health forums and invite the community to come and listen to our presentations? That was so awesome."

"Slowly the staff started coming and listening to our presentations, and saw that we wanted to improve our health inside and outside prison."

"They saw us I think for the first time as real people and not just inmates."

"There was a huge change in the guards, being more friendly, not all about the power trip."

"One of the women created her first crystal meth power point presentation and was asked to do a staff training."

"It blew one of the staff members away!"

"And afterwards the two of them sat down and talked to each other."

"It was the day I think this staff did a full circle. This staff member was previously very black and white. She changed as a result of this."

"One of the local high schools heard about the research we were doing inside the prison and thought it would be great to bring us into the high school to teach Grade 10 to 12 students. So a couple of the women went, shared their PowerPoints, and their stories about being addicted to drugs and what happened to them."

"When the women came back they were on cloud nine from the response the students gave them."

Community

When I returned to my hometown, my house had been turned into a crack shack. I didn't want to go back to that lifestyle; I didn't want to go back to jail. But I couldn't get welfare, and I didn't know how to get a job. So, I went back to what I knew— selling drugs. Eight weeks later, I was back in jail. No one who worked at the jail was surprised that I was back so fast. Jail was the only place I felt safe or belonged. I figured this was all my life would be.

–Mo Korchinski

Paragraphs of Passion

J

My passion is women's health rights.

K

My passion is first and second stage housing. It is the one and only way to success for women who leave jail.

L

My passion is to help women and kids gain the knowledge of what drugs do to your life. I want to share the effects that drugs had on me.

M

My passion is to learn more about crystal meth and its effects on our health, and to help increase awareness of the dangers of this drug.

N

Phobias, specifically social phobia. I have always had trouble dealing with large groups of people and individuals in new situations. I have seen the effects of this in my life. I have begun to deal with this issue but I still have fear of ridicule.

O

One passion is recovery in the family. I am a recovering addict and my mother is as well. I find it easier to cope when I have someone who is going through the same thing, to deal with it together, to be stronger by combining both of our powers to prevail and recover.

P

As a feminist, I have observed that women are served poorly by our justice system. So many lawyers treat women caught up in addictions with barely concealed contempt and I'm told most of the judges women appear before, whether male or female, are of the same opinion. I would like to broaden my research to include the use of court ordered injunctions to frighten and intimidate women.

Doctor's Journey

RUTH ELWOOD MARTIN

TODAY'S PRISON HEALTH RESEARCH FORUM was attended by representatives from eight community health organizations, including people from Fraser Health Authority. Also, a reporter from the local newspaper interviewed Debra Hanson about her passion to create supportive housing for women from prison. Debra was so thrilled! I find it so encouraging that people from community health and advocacy organizations are willing to provide their support to women when they leave prison.

— Journal entry

The World Health Organization advocates the principle of community equivalence: incarcerated individuals should have access to health programs equivalent to those in the community, in accordance with standard minimum rules for the treatment of prisoners (First UN Congress). "Prison services, their supporting health programmes ... must increase their coverage and attain the standard of care available to free citizens in the community," according to one medical journal editorial (Levy 511). Another leading medical journal stated that incarcerated individuals are out of reach of conventional community-based health systems and should be provided with community equivalent health services in order to improve the public health of the population (Fazel and Baillargeon 962).

The right to health extends beyond access to health-care services and includes a wide range of factors that can help us lead a healthy life, otherwise known as meeting the "underlying determinants of health." These include gender equality, adequate nutrition and housing, healthy working and environmental conditions, health-related education, and information (Office of the UN). A powerful illustration of the provision of the "right to health" factors for prison inmates is Kiran Bedi's description of her tenure as director of a vast network of prisons in India. By inviting NGOs and community agencies to partner with her, Bedi was able to offer rehabilitative, therapeutic and health promotion services to incarcerated men and women, their families, and correctional staff—something that would not otherwise have been possible within her correctional budget or mandate.

Of the nine health goals arising from the participatory health research project (Martin et al.), at least seven required engagement of outside organizations in order for women to achieve them, including the attainment of safe and stable housing and acquiring meaningful work. In addition, for women transitioning from life inside prison to life on the outside, engagement with the outside community would facilitate their continuity of educational opportunities, employment training, supportive housing, and health-care services.

For women in prison, engagement with the outside community should and could begin inside prison prior to their release. Relationships that women establish with community organizations while they are inside prison can assist them during their transition to the outside world. This chapter bears witness to the importance of correctional institutions building bridges with community: community organizations came into the prison to share their expertise with the prison, and these resultant bridges facilitated women's transition into the community upon their release.

REFERENCES

Bedi, K. *It's Always Possible: Transforming One of the Largest Prisons in the World.* New Delhi: Stirling Paperbacks, 2006.

Fazel, S. and J. Baillargeon. "The Health of Prisoners." *Lancet* 377 (9769) (2011): 956-65.

First United Nations Congress. "Standard Minimum Rules for the Treatment of Prisoners." Geneva: United Nations, 1955.

Levy, M. " "Prison Health Services." *British Medical Journal* 315 (1997):1394-5.

Martin, R. Elwood, et al. "The Development of Participatory Health Research Among Incarcerated Women in a Canadian Prison." *International Journal of Prisoner Health* 5 (2) (2009): 95-107.

Office of the United Nations High Commissioner for Human Rights. "The Right to Health." Factsheet 31. Geneva: WHO, 2008.

Working Together
Prison in the Community and the Community in Prison

MO KORCHINSKI

THE PRISON STARTED TO WORK with the community and the community started to work with the prison. Job placements allowed women to work for local businesses. For me, the one big thing that I got out of going to prison was having a purpose. In prison, I had a job, a voice that was listened to. I had meaning in my day to day living. I didn't have healthy choices on the outside of prison but I did inside. I couldn't seem to find my place in society. I didn't know how to break the barrier from the addictive life style to becoming a productive member of a community. Having women go out into the community and build self-esteem and a sense of belonging was very powerful for many women. One of the job placements was working at a second hand clothing store in the community, where women worked in the back room sorting and hanging clothes, but only a few women qualified for security clearance to be permitted to work outside the gates each day. So between the second hand store and the prison, the clothing was brought to the prison so other women could help with the sorting and hanging of clothes. This helped more women to find a purpose and feel that they were doing something meaningful.

Working with the SPCA, walking dogs, or helping clean out the kennels, was another job in the community. The prison started a dog daycare for staff to drop their dogs off. We ended up fostering a dog named Chase who was born with health problems and needed an operation. We kept Chase for months until the surgery was completed and he could be adopted. We sold ice-cream to raise money to help fund Chase's surgery, and the prison matched what we raised.

The high school asked if the women at ACCW would be interested in helping with the Grade 12 graduation by making the centrepieces for the grad dinner. We set up the arts and crafts room as a workshop and made 250 centrepieces. When the teacher came to the prison to see

153

how we were doing, a health forum was in process. She was curious about the forum, asking what was happening. I explained how women researched areas of interest, such as drug addiction and related health issues. She asked if any members of the prison research team would be willing to come speak to the high school students about their research. A date and time was set up, and a team of women went to present at the high school to a full auditorium of teenagers. This interaction was another positive connection to the community. The community started to see us as women, not as delinquents or criminals.

Hope

MO KORCHINSKI

hopeless
my life
hope
to die
hopeless
getting busted
hope
charges will be dropped
hopeless
going to court
hope
for short sentence
hopeless
off to jail
hope
for ACCW
hopeless
turns to hope
hope
turns to healing

Women on the
Prison Research Team Debrief

THROUGHOUT THE COURSE of the prison participatory research project, the women on the research team explored and experienced many "firsts"—for example, using a computer or creating a PowerPoint presentation, presenting research findings to an audience, or writing a letter to a community agency. Following these "firsts," the team would take time to debrief with each other about how they were feeling. They often recorded and transcribed their debriefing conversations, knowing that these "firsts" were historical moments and might someday be of value.

A particularly emotional "first" was when the local high school invited women of the prison health research team to give a health education forum about drugs and alcohol for the Grade 10 students. After the high school forum was finished, the women returned to prison, sat in the research room, and debriefed the experience. The debriefing conversation was particularly poignant that day; as evidenced by the following portion of that conversation:

"I was really moved. My aim was to touch just one student and I know I did. Our stories; it's so powerful. We are all from jail and we have the same stories. I was moved by it."

"When I presented my life story today, it was the first time I heard my own words and I looked up and saw those kids. They were listening, hanging onto my every word and I felt that was great. I was letting those kids into my own world, hoping I touched just one of them. Today I know my word had an effect and I am proud of it."

"One student reminded me of when I first started doing drugs. She cried and said, 'my brother passed away, committed suicide, jumped off a bridge.' I started crying, she was crying. It was very sad. It made me realize how lucky I am."

"There's stuff I've been holding on to with my life. For instance my fiancé being out there—I don't know if he is going to wait for me. I'm really emotional; I went for parole last week and was denied. I'm having a difficult time holding my feelings in. I have beautiful children and their parents are not there for them."

"I was sexually abused by a family member and I was at war with myself. I locked it away and at the age of twenty-five I was having an intimate moment with a boyfriend and it just came out. Finally, at the age of twenty-eight, I can say I loved my brother. I'm not angry, I'm angry at his actions but not with him. I found peace. Coming to jail I've found I am more at peace with myself and the world. I am happy. I can talk about it openly and explain things to people. Because I thought it was my fault. That's why I wouldn't go to anyone. So if I can speak openly about it then maybe other people can."

"I've been in denial about a lot of things in life, but talking to the students at the school woke me up. I have children at that age. I wished my son or daughter was in there to hear what I had to say because I didn't know how to approach my kids or how to talk to them about drugs. Seeing their expressions, they were in awe of all the information we were giving them. It's all the information I had soaked up in this research group. I've learned quite a bit. Now I can go home and give some back to my children."

"We came together today as a group and did it and I am proud of us. I hope they looked at those pictures, heard what we said, and are going to think about it. Our stories were real and I feel a sense of pride of our group as a whole."

"What I really liked about the research group is I got to spend a lot of time sharing. If I was on the outside I would not do this. If I can help just one person it was worth it. The research team made me a new person."

"I've been to the forums in the prison and today in the high school, and you are amazing. You are very professional in your presentations. It was really cool to see students coming back into the theatre wanting to meet you and learn more from you. You did amazing work" (prison nurse).

Writing Letters in Prison to the Outside Community

PARTICIPATORY HEALTH RESEARCH involves social action or change. Women in prison realized that to effect system change they needed to connect with people or agencies (that is, outside community) that might listen and respond by improving policy or creating interventions. However, communication with the outside world is limited for incarcerated women, because they have no Internet access and phone calls are costly. Therefore, the women on the prison research team practised and honed their letter writing skills.

We share with you next two letters, out of scores of letters written by women on the research team to community organizations.

Letter by Lisa Torikka

My name is Lisa Torikka and I am incarcerated at ACCW in Maple Ridge, BC. This is my third incarceration in the last two years (first sentence nine months, second and third six months). My addiction has been relatively short compared to most addicts I know. When I am in jail, I do not use drugs, I have regular contact with my father, and I do wonderful things within our prison community, not only for myself but also for the women presently in jail and the others to come. I have completed nine computer courses in jail, built a labyrinth (out of 3,329 rocks), attend native sisterhood and sweats, and really worked on my spirituality and inner growth. I work very hard at any job I do and am currently working outside the gates three to four times a week at a thrift store, the SPCA, and a horse ranch for terminally ill children. So, why is it that I have such a hard time continuing my success outside of these prison walls?

My addiction to drugs is my problem. And I do not have a safe place to go after I finish my sentence. Every time I am released, I intend to go to a recovery house or a treatment centre, but instead, I go right back to the Downtown Eastside, my home for the last seven years.

We need a safe place to go to plan the rest of our lives, finish school, get a job.

I am going to be released from prison and have a safe place to go to. I have high hopes for my continued success at sobriety on "the outs" and I am very optimistic about my future. I have no intentions of going back to the Eastside when I am released and I am very lucky to have a safe place to go, but others are not. Instead, they pick up where they left off, for lack of a safe place to go. I want to stay clean and I know that I require support when I leave here.

We need help. I think that with a collective effort between Corrections, communities, and inmates, we can build safe environments for women to successfully reintegrate into society. A proposal is in the works for second and third stage housing for women out of prison, through a unique research project that is currently taking place at ACCW with Dr. Ruth Martin, our prison doctor. Hopefully we will get the houses we need so that we can stop the "revolving door" of prison. I am developing a website for this research project so that women who are released from prison can benefit from the efforts of women inside prison walls and stay connected to the work we have started. I thank you for your time and please wish me and all the other inmates luck as we get out of prison with the few resources we have to survive in our communities.

Letter written to Amnesty International by Renee Chan

Hello and Greetings from the Alouette Correctional Centre for Women. My name is Renee Chan. I am the Inmate Committee Coordinator.

I would like to tell you a little about our prison, and how I became interested in your organization, and what I am hoping to achieve by involving Amnesty International in our community.

This prison is like no other. It is not perfect and we share common ground with most prisons, yet we realize that we are freer here than we have ever been, and that we are on a healing journey.

My role as inmate coordinator is to be on top of any inmate concerns and to be the voice of our community to the line staff, management, Citizens Advisory Board, and to the wardens. I write proposals, advocate for support for women on their healing journey, offer peer support, and organize fundraising activities (we donate raised money to the community and sponsor families at Christmas). Our committee is self-supporting through fundraising and bead sales, an inmate run sale of paper products and beading materials. We pay for our own cable and newspapers.

I am looking for ways to get women involved, not only with our "little society," but also with the larger, global society. After seeing a program about Amnesty International, I wondered what we could do to help. We are interested in having one paying member, Alison Granger-Brown, our recreation therapist. Would it be okay if the other four members changed from time to time? We would also like to incorporate programs about the pleas of others, on a regular educational basis. As inmates we are allowed seven free letters to be sent out per week, and are able to hold writing circles. The powers that be are very excited that we would like to take on this venture. I feel that if letters could come from inside our prison walls to the powers that be at other prisons, demanding the respect, dignity, and fair treatment of others, that would be powerful. We have fought for our rights, and continue to do so every day in a respectful way. I also feel that it would be therapeutic for the women to feel that they are in some way "giving back."

Last week another community organization, Joint Effort, came in with materials to help to build a banner for the Memorial March, for missing and murdered women. The response was great and time that was spent exchanging stories, offering support, and just learning what it was like to be women, touched many of us. We love to be able to be part of these types of events, including Prisoners Justice Day, World Aids Day, and National Violence Against Women Day. It is helpful for us, to get out of our problems and daily complaints and issues to remember those who truly suffer. We enjoy it.

I am hoping that I have somehow given you some knowledge into ACCW, *and how we really are advanced through hard work and dedication on the part of both staff and ourselves. It truly is through working together that we are able to initiate growth, and then change. I look forward to hearing from you and Amnesty soon.*

Sincerely,

Renee Chan,
Inmate Committee Coordinator

W2W Community Reaching In, Reaching Out

LINNEA GROOM

T HE "W2W" IS A WOMAN TO WOMAN PROGRAM sponsored by M2/ W2 Association. It has long been recognized that women and men inside correctional institutions are frequently estranged from family and community, and have minimal support systems. In response to their need for social connections, M2/W2 came into being in the mid 1960s, sending volunteers from the faith community into prison to visit with inmates and form one-on-one mentoring relationships.

It has been my privilege to coordinate the W2 program at ACCW from the time it opened. I assign (match) a "W2W" to visit with a specific woman. These W2 relationships provide opportunities for different kinds of conversations than are typical in the prison: emotionally safe conversations with people of different perspectives, who aren't struggling with many of the issues that their fellow inmates are, or prison staff who have power over them. W2 volunteers are non-judgmental and encouraging. Sometimes these are the first positive relationships inmates have had in their lives. Incarcerated women often have huge problems with trust, yet the W2 relationship allows for the opportunity to build a trusting relationship with someone, which in turn is a precursor for a relationship that also includes accountability and responsibility.

I watch a tiny spark of hope being nurtured as I observe these relationships develop "inside" and often continue as a source of both support and accountability on the "outside."

During my last stint at ACCW, I decided to sign up for a W2 worker; we used to call them 'rent a friend.' Every other week, one of these nice Christian ladies would come and talk to us and listen to our heartaches, our hopes and dreams, even our lies and our pitfalls. My W2 worker directed me to a supportive housing facility for women living in the community. The woman who ran this house was also a W2 volunteer. She was a small person, funny and outspoken. When she played guitar, many of the women were moved to tears. I left prison and moved into her house, rather ambivalent about the Christian lifestyle. I moved in saying I would stay three months and ended up living there for over three years. I lived there because I felt loved, respected, and nurtured. All it takes is one person to believe in us, to love us in order for us to flourish and feel safe enough to change.

— Kelly Murphy

Something's Happening
Behind the Barbed Wire Fence

TERRY HOWARD

THE FRONT GATES looked like those of any other prison I visited over the ten years I was a prison outreach worker. But the chain link fence with barbed wire "hairdo" was the only thing that dispelled the illusion that this was just another little motel complex in the middle of a rural park. Pressing the intercom on the door of the gate resulted in a cheery voice asking, "How can I help you?" Entering the gate, coming through an electronically locked heavy metal door, and being greeted by a uniformed woman behind thick glass asking for my ID and keys made me remember I was visiting a BC Correctional Centre for Women where female prisoners sentenced to "two years, less a day" were incarcerated.

My outreach activities involved providing support to prisoners living with HIV/AIDS, through education, advocacy, health-care assistance, and HIV-related counselling. From my first visit to the Alouette Correctional Centre for Women, I felt a tangible difference in the atmosphere from the men's correctional centres I also visited in my role as an outreach worker. The feeling was one of a healing lodge, or a place of rehabilitation, rather than simply housing for convicted criminals. As an outreach worker, I immediately appreciated the difference in atmosphere and noticed staff and prisoners alike smiling as I passed them en route to my regular meeting place. I was impressed by the courtesy and respect shown to the women by the staff. The women also showed respect to the staff when asking for access to buildings, program related materials, and when responding to intercom requests for their attendance. Flowers were planted along walkways, lawns tended, and a beautiful memorial rock garden was constructed by, and for the women living in the centre. It was obvious that the women felt responsible for nurturing their surroundings and the sense of purpose they embodied during their incarceration in this place.

None of the women I worked with had any illusion about the fact they were in a prison. Despite the beautiful surroundings, a prison still has locked doors and highly restricted freedom. The healing lodge approach to incarceration at the centre provided many with an opportunity to reflect on which events in their lives had led to criminal activity, and many women were attempting to change the often lifelong and generational patterns that resulted in their incarceration. Many made a decision to work on improving their circumstances, and use the time in prison to heal and develop coping skills to aid them on the outside.

One of the most remarkable examples that I have ever witnessed of how this change in the overall climate of the ACCW affected the women was during the initial stages of the Prison Participatory Health Research project. When the women were asked to write a paragraph of passion about an issue that was important to them, their diversity came through. Women wrote about HIV, hepatitis, shop-lifting, self-mutilation (cutting), and many more issues they experienced first-hand. They were asked to develop a presentation to outside visitors who would be invited in to view the presentations, and for the other women in the prison to learn from. They received full support from the warden, Brenda Tole, who understood and witnessed the transformation of women engaged in meaningful work that benefited themselves, as well as the larger community. The warden allowed the women previously forbidden access to the Internet to research their paragraph of passion topic, and to gather information for their presentations. The increase in library use, reading and writing workshop attendance, and my own outreach appointments were at an all time high as the women gathered material for their upcoming presentations.

When the presentations were ready, the women very proudly spoke in front of invited members of the public. Some reluctantly at first, but then gaining steam as they saw the overwhelmingly positive reception from the invited guests.

I was stunned at the new passion to pass on the information from their presentations to the other women incarcerated with them in an informal, yet incredibly effective educational blitz. In my ten years of prison outreach, I had never seen an uptake of information as effective as what happened between my bi-weekly visits to the centre among the women with their newfound knowledge of the power of education. They were passionate, informed, and intent on letting other women know of the dangers inherent in their own issue.

The high level of accuracy of the information as a result of Internet and library access, and the peer-driven education initiative had a dramatic noticeable influence on the self-esteem of the women. This, in my opinion, resulted in a marked decline in security issues (violence), an increase in requests for/attendance at health-care appointments, and a wonderful warm sense of camaraderie among the women that replaced the overarching sense of punishment that hung in the air at every prison I've ever visited.

During my regular outreach visits with the women living with HIV/ AIDS, I noticed a difference in the sheer number and the nature of the questions I was asked. They changed from the immediate concerns about how long someone with HIV could live, to thoughtful inquiries on medication options, how to stay healthy, and requests for information on addiction treatment and harm reduction tools. The basic level of knowledge of HIV/AIDS had risen.

A new knowledge-induced tolerance among the women resulted in a decrease in HIV stigma related behaviours, like toilet segregation and hurtful messaging for women living with HIV, which had been a huge source of fear for HIV+ women in the past. I learned that peer-education was an immensely powerful tool in a closed setting like prison, and one that reached farther into the community than I could ever hope for with conventional educational methods.

I was able to share this information with correctional health-care policy-makers and other community outreach workers, attempting to effect change in the way we conduct outreach education and learning from the experience I observed during this highly controversial project. Not all my information was well received, and critics still retort, "prison is not supposed to be a country club." The gift I was given from observing the women during this project, and the corresponding increase in successful outcomes of my outreach work, was well worth the effort to share the experience and endure the "soft on crime" criticism I received.

Indigenous Learning

I didn't know anything about the Aboriginal culture and spirituality, but I learnt it at Holy Cow's sweats and her meetings. And when girls would come back to jail she would not judge them, she would say, "There are more lessons for you to learn."

—Christine Hemingway

Paragraphs of Passion

Q

My passion is Aboriginal rights for women. There has been so much abuse in Native families. Natives need to share not only culture and religion with people; we need to share our hurts as well.

R

My passion is Aboriginal studies. I am Native and my mother is very involved in her culture. My mother is very important to me, and her acceptance is major to my life.

S

My passion is spirituality because I believe that it can improve a person's physical, mental, and emotional state whatever it may be.

T

I have always had great interests in language and I enjoy working with adults with literacy challenges. This is an area that I would like to continue to work on as being literate is a way to autonomy and self-growth.

U

My passion is to help other Aboriginal women better understand their culture and language and open up people's mind and hearts to the beauty of the Aboriginal ways and life style. I also want to research the ministry's dealing with children and sex trade apprehension.

V

I have many passions, I have experienced many things. I would love to do Aboriginal studies.

Doctor's Journey

RUTH ELWOOD MARTIN

THIS EVENING, WHEN I FINISHED WORK, I stepped out of the clinic door into the cool, crisp, evening air. The moon had just risen above the dark forest skyline and the throb of the drumming drew me, pulsating, from the Eagle Hut. I walked across the grass lawn and paused in the hut doorway, watching the women sitting around the drum, intent as they coordinated their drum strokes, singing as if their hearts would break. And, then, all of the women in the hut rose to a stand, joining together in unison, loud as if singing out across the universe, singing for all women, for strength and for wisdom. It seemed to me that they had completely forgotten their troubled lives; they were singing from a place of fulfillment and purpose. I wished that they could share this moment, their singing and their beauty, with the whole world.
—Journal entry

The fastest growing segment of the federal corrections population is that representing women of ethnic minorities. From 1998 to 2008, the number of federally sentenced Aboriginal peoples increased 20 percent, with incarceration of Aboriginal women increasing dramatically by 131 percent (Mann). The magnitude of this over-representation is particularly high in Ontario and the western and prairie provinces, with rates ranging between five to ten times the expected prevalence rates (La Prairie). In BC, on any day, up to 40 percent of women in provincial institutions are Aboriginal.

Culturally responsive prison health allows us to hear what Aboriginal people have been telling us—that patterns of criminal behaviour are often an expression of the trauma, pain, anger, and grief, experienced by Aboriginal peoples as a consequence of their history of residential school abuses and/or dispossession. This is related to substance use, intergenerational abuse, low levels of education, employment and income, poor housing, and poor access to health care (Howell; Krieg). Although progress has been made, many of the 200 actionable items outlined in the 2006 Strategic Plan for Aboriginal Corrections have not yet been implemented (Mann).

The 2007 Tripartite First Nations Health Plan in BC recognized that:

> Health and wellness for First Nations encompasses the physical, spiritual, mental, economic, emotional, environmental, social and cultural wellness of the individual, family and community.... The way forward will require a joint commitment to deal with the root causes and structural issues causing socio-economic gaps. (Tripartite First Nations Health Plan 3)

A similar model could be adopted for governing the health care for all incarcerated Canadian people, given the vast over-representation of Aboriginal peoples in our prisons.

I learned from women in prison about their history of residential school abuses. Women in prison who are my age or older were forcibly separated as young children from their parents, homes, language, and culture, to live in residential schools. Their mental, emotional, spiritual, and physical health bears the brunt of their traumatic residential school childhood experiences. The younger women were raised by parents who, as children, were torn from their family, community, and culture; these younger women's health is also impacted by the generational legacy of residential schools.

The term "health literacy" is used to describe the ability to access, understand, and act on information for health. Accessing health information and services can be very difficult for incarcerated women, particularly Aboriginal women, because of their repeated experiences of discrimination, stigma, and consequent distrust. Being able to access, understand, and integrate information about health makes a difference to incarcerated women's health and well-being.

On one occasion, an Aboriginal woman joined the prison health research team; she was an Elder in her home community and a residential school survivor. It had taken her several weeks to join the team because of her distrust of officials such as physicians. She would listen, quietly beading intricate jewellery as we talked, and offering only a few words of advice or comment during the research team's discussions. One of the younger women worked with her to create a PowerPoint presentation about the family legend of Ts'il?os and ?Eniyud (Mt. Tatlow and Waddington); for the prison health research forum, she told the legend in her language of Xeni Gwet'in and then translated it into English. Just before she left prison, she placed one of her beaded necklaces around my neck with the promise, "Dr. Martin, we'll make an injun of you yet!"

Through the prison participatory research project, I learned from Aboriginal women that health is comprised of intertwined and inter-dependent facets: mental, emotional, spiritual, and physical. One of the health goals identified by women inside prison was to integrate healthy living into one's life. For all women inside prison, regardless of ethnicity, this health goal became translated into 'learning how to integrate emotional, mental, physical and spiritual healthy practices into one's life.'

Brenda Tole invited an Aboriginal Elder, Mary Fayant, known to everyone as Holy Cow, to bring Aboriginal teachings and practice to the women, regardless of their heritage. Holy Cow was a source of inspiration and counsel for the women. In these pages, we bear witness to the stories of Mo and other women who learned from Holy Cow the teachings of Aboriginal ways of being in the world. In addition, Lara-Lisa Condello of Nicola Valley Institute of Technology (NVIT) met with Brenda, and participated in several prison health research forums. Lara-Lisa shares with us her narrative of teaching a course on indigenous ways of knowing with women in prison who proved to be eager and insightful students.

REFERENCES

Howell, T. *The Point of No Return: Aboriginal Offenders' Journey Towards a Crime Free Life.* Unpublished dissertation. University of British Columbia, Vancouver, 2008.

Krieg, A. S. "Aboriginal Incarceration: Health and Social Impacts." *The Medical Journal of Australi*a 184 (10) (2006): 534-6.

La Prairie, C. "Aboriginal Over-representation in the Criminal Justice System: A Tale of Nine Cities." *Canadian Journal of Criminology/ Revue canadienne de criminologie* 44 (2) (2002): 181-208.

Mann, M. M. "Good Intentions, Disappointing Results: A Progress Report on Federal Aboriginal Corrections." Office of the Correctional Investigator, 2010. Web.

Tripartite First Nations Health Plan. Signed by the First Nations Leadership Council, the Government of Canada and the Government of BC, 2007. Web.

Sacred Rhythm

MO KORCHINSKI

Thump Thump
Thump Thump
sacred rhythm
begins to beat
Against elk and tree
Thump Thump
Thump Thump
all sharing one thing
Heart beat of prison
songs from our hearts
Healing the past
Thump Thump
Thump Thump
all related one way or another
the streets of Vancouver to hills of Kelowna
mountains that sit high in the north
heart that beats
heart of the drum
Thump Thump
Thump Thump
power of sound carries us all

Moving together spirit above

Creating our path

follow this beat

Thump Thump
Thump Thump

I first went to prison in 2005 and I remember the pizza days and the sweats. It felt like I was at home because of the cultural aspect. I never thought I would go to jail and have Holy Cow honour me. She put her hands on my shoulders and said, "Just because your parents aren't alive, it doesn't mean that they didn't love you because they did love you." Inside the Eagle Hut, there was an unspoken level of respect. She taught us that when you walked into the hut, you left the stuff at the door, and that inside the Eagle Hut you learnt respect for each other and the cultural traditions.

—Marnie Scow

Holy Cow taught us to leave our problems outside the walls of the prison, to leave the street life behind. She taught us that everyone deserves to be heard and to be treated equally with compassion and understanding.

—Mo Korchinski

Research Forum, Prayer[1]

ABORIGINAL ELDER, MARIE FAYANT, HOLY COW

I want to thank you all who came here today. I would also like to thank our ancestors, whose territory we are on.

It's good to see that the community are coming in to help support our women and give them the hope that they need to get healthy in the four aspects: mental, spiritual, physical, and emotional.

These women need your help and I believe you also need their help for these are our future grandmothers, who will be teaching our children.

So if we don't start the healing process, then the healing will not begin on the outside. It will just be a vicious circle. We need to break the cycle, to help our women get healthy.

All My Relations

[1]Holy Cow shared this prayer at the opening of the day-long research forum in October, 2005, which marked the start of the prison health research project.

Aboriginal Healing in Prison

MO KORCHINSKI

THE PRISON CONTRACTED AN ABORIGINAL ELDER, Holy Cow, to come into the prison and to teach us about spirituality and the Aboriginal ways. Holy Cow taught us to leave our problems outside the walls of the prison, to leave the street life behind. She taught us that everyone deserves to be heard and to be treated with compassion and understanding.

Elders use traditional Aboriginal healing methods to help Aboriginal and non-Aboriginal people heal from the effects of alcohol and drug abuse. Holy Cow came into the prison three days a week. Tuesday and Thursday nights, we would gather for singing and drumming in the Eagle Hut, which is a round building in the centre of the prison, heated by a wood stove. On Sunday, if it was not raining and if there was no fire ban in the area, we would have a sweat ceremony on the sweat grounds. Sweat lodge ceremonies are also called purification sweats. During sweat lodge ceremonies, you may experience rebirth. For those who struggle with addiction or alcoholism, the spiritual experience of rebirth can be freeing from a past of addiction and crime. The feeling of rebirth, reawakening, and renewal are palpable after a sweat.

The frame of the sweat lodge is built from willow branches, and the lodge is built once a year. The job of going out and cutting the willows is left up to the Elder, who teaches us how to build the sweat lodge. We always seem to build the sweat lodge too tall as Holy Cow says that we have "built a sky scraper not a sweat lodge." Before you can cover the lodge you must lay down blankets, which go around the hole that has been dug for the stones to go in. This task is normally done by the women who are called the ground keepers. The outside of the lodge is covered with tarps and blankets, which overlap one and another as to not let any sunlight seep through any holes or spaces. During this time the Fire Keeper starts the fire and heats the forty stones, or grandfathers.

179

As the fire heats the stones, the last touches are given to the lodge to protect it and those who are to enter.

As the fire keeper is looking after the fire, everyone going into the sweat Lodge must make prayer ties. Prayer ties are made from a small coloured square piece of material to which you add a small amount of tobacco. Prayer ties are coloured in black, red, yellow, and white. Each colour represents one part of the self: spiritual, physical, emotional, and mental. It is very important that you stay focused on positive, healing prayers and energy while making your prayer ties and speaking your prayers with each prayer tie you make. Prayer ties are spiritual focusing tools used by Aboriginal peoples. They are considered a physical offering and representation to carry the energy of prayers to the Creator and Spirit World. The making of prayer ties is ceremonious. It should be done with reverence and treated as sacred.

Holy Cow was here tonight. The Eagle Hut was so packed with women that we ran out of chairs and women were sitting on the floor. Going to the Eagle Hut is a nice break and gives me time to connect with a sense of spirituality that I never knew. Today, six women sat around the drum drumming and singing as others sat in a circle around the drum singing as one. Holy Cow is amazing—the strength that she has and the power of hope she has for all of us. The non-judgemental attitude Holy Cow has towards all of us and how much her belief in each of us is healing.

Aboriginal Elder in Prison

ABORIGINAL ELDER, MARIE FAYANT, HOLY COW

First, I would like to acknowledge the First Peoples of these territories for allowing me to live and work in their territories.

My role as a Spiritual Advisor is to provide services to women in prison for their mental, spiritual, physical, and emotional well-being. These include sweat ceremonies, pipe ceremonies, healing circles, cultural teachings, and counselling, as well as beading, making shawls, making drums, singing, and dancing. Through the ways of our ancestors' teachings, the women inmates find their way back to their own culture. They learn about their people, so that they have the courage to go back to their families with dignity and respect.

It is very important to understand what our Aboriginal women's needs are health-wise to heal in a traditional way and have our traditional foods of the territories. Along with more needed services.

Thank you, All My Relations.

Building Bridges with Women
in the Spirit of Learning

LARA-LISA CONDELLO

I AM BLESSED TO WORK for an Aboriginal post-secondary institution that supports women in prison as full members of our community. My journey in British Columbia prisons over twelve years has blossomed into a deeper understanding of transformative justice and participatory community-based practices.

This journey began in my childhood. I have learned from my Elders that all things are interrelated, and although there are four stages of life, we venture back to the east many times in our life to reflect and renew our spirits. The east represents our sense of protection, innocence, hope, trust, and spontaneity (Lane, Bopp, Bopp, and Brown). We learn here to love with non-judgment and uncritical acceptance. The east also represents courage, truth, and leadership. I believe our collective journey at ACCW began in the east, which is the place of all beginnings.

My relationship with ACCW began in August 2006, when two former colleagues and I came to understand, as prison advocates, that prison is a micro-cosmos of our society. How we choose to treat the most underserving and marginalized reflects who we are as a people. Too many times, we forget the simple fact that women who are incarcerated are mothers, sisters, daughters, and friends, and that they will return to their communities one day.

We arrived at the prison gates and the warden, Brenda Tole, warmly welcomed us. I remember my first impression of Brenda. She was accessible, transparent, and spoke in common and candid language. She said, the prison was not working, the doors were revolving, and it was necessary for us to work together to build positive change for the women. Under Brenda's leadership, the prison was very open to the community and to possibilities for education.

The motivation and momentum to open the prison to community

members who could offer relevant and meaningful programming for the women was luminous, sincere, and almost contagious. Our participatory engagement and transparent communications guided us into a flexible, yet integral process. My learning was braided with others' interpretations and understandings of the world and our learning was driven by the power of the collective.

Between 2007 and 2010, over 100 women participated in our *Building Bridges for Women: Community Reintegration Through Education* program. I worked with many young women who were under-educated: approximately, 60 percent of the women had a Grade 10 level education or less, and 25 percent of the women had experienced some kind of post-secondary education, mainly first and second year courses. Only two percent reported any kind of trades training. The women shared diverse learning styles, with 26 percent reporting learning best through experiential activities, 15 percent were visual learners, ten percent enjoyed working in groups, and ten percent found oral learning very important. Four percent and one percent of the women reported enjoying learning through written work and computer work, respectively.

When asked to articulate their learning expectations, half of the group wanted to learn about their culture, 30 percent simply wanted to be in a learning environment, and seven percent recorded growth as their personal expectations. The women shared their hopes and dreams. Every woman wanted to give back to her family and community, and 30 percent of the women reported career aspirations of working in schools, 26 percent wanted to work in social services and 19 percent in health care. The women innately knew that by sharing their voices, others could learn from their lived experiences and healing journeys. There was hope and resiliency in their stories of despair and marginalization.

In short, *Building Bridges* offered educational opportunities for women in prison designed to:

- Enhance Aboriginal social, economic, cultural and political knowledge;
- Promote the learning, health and overall well-being of Aboriginal women; and
- Celebrate the diversity and richness of Aboriginal cultures and languages in Canada.

Perhaps it was not what we were learning, but how we learned together that made a difference. What was unique about *Building Bridges?*

First, our classroom in prison encouraged the free expression and practice of Aboriginal values and ways of being. Our program was guided by an indigenous philosophical concept of holism (Archibald) that draws on honouring the interrelationships between one's intellectual, spiritual, emotional, and physical self.

Secondly, the program was rooted in collaborative learning and transformative justice. Both paradigms alter traditional positions and power relationships. I asked the women to identify their own motivations to learn. We engaged in interpersonal and teamwork in the classroom to cultivate skills of active listening, reflective thought, and critical evaluation of complex issues. I encouraged the women to clarify their positions and act on their personal values through their stories and narratives. Women were told less and were asked to discover their own interpretations of course concepts and discussions. Everyone had an opportunity to engage in peer feedback, ask each other questions, and draw on their personal experiences. We shared goals while respecting the position of others and the process of dialogue. Active participation, responsibility, and accountability from all parties were hallmarks of our collaborative classroom. We drew on the power of our collective knowledge.

Third, we valued experiential activities and the use of art in our classroom. I have come to see art as a tool that supports the exploration of sensitive topics and our personal learning journeys in the classroom. Women were encouraged to share their passions through artistic, oral, or written expressions.

Fourth, I found that I could not ask my students to value their voices and understand who they are without doing the same for myself. Critical challenges and discussions were appreciated in our classroom; change, risk, and complexities were valued. The women in prison taught me to challenge and deconstruct notions of who I should be or perhaps who others want me to be, and to focus on my own volition and vision.

My journey has evolved into a very personal questioning of who I am as a woman, who I want to become and how I am interrelated to others. So often we define ourselves by what we do, not by who we are or by the ways we are in the world. At ACCW, I came to understand learning as an opportunity to broaden the mind and open the spirit.

REFERENCES

Archibald, J. Q'um Q'um Xiiem. *Indigenous Storywork: Educating the Heart, Mind, Body, and Spirit.* Vancouver: University of British Columbia Press, 2008.

Bopp, J., P. Lane, L. Brown, and M. Bopp. *The Sacred Tree : Reflections on Native American Spirituality.* Twin Lakes, WI: Lotus Press, 1984. Print.

Leaving Holy Cow Style

MO KORCHINSKI

THE RITUALS THAT HOLY COW and the women hold for the women who are released are empowering for all involved. When women are leaving the prison, we pray and sing out the women who are being released in the morning. Singing out is singing and praying for the women before they go back out into the real world of life. We do this by lining up in two lines facing each other and holding hands. Women who are getting released start off in between the arms of the first pair of women.

One by one, each woman says her goodbye and tells the woman to be released what one of her strengths is and that she can make it on the outside. This ritual goes on until every woman in the Eagle Hut has spoken words of encouragement.

The last time I was sung out was bittersweet. I knew that I had learned everything I needed to learn from Holy Cow and that I would miss her and the other women. Standing in between women you feel are your family and listening to them tell you your strengths is very emotional and it can be hard to believe that they are talking about you. Walking out the door of the Eagle Hut for the last time brought back many memories, tears, laughter, and much healing. What I have learned will be with me for the rest of my life.

My Longest Journey

LARA-LISA CONDELLO

*I offer this writing in honour of the women who opened and shared
their spirit with creation upon our learning journey in prison.*

In the Spirit of Learning,

The longest journey I will travel is the twelve inches
between my head and heart.
A medicine man once shared this gift with me
as he warmly welcomed me in into his blanket ceremony.
It was dark and lonely as I was wrapped in the heavy wool.
I began to think of all the women who support me in my life-long
journey as I listened to my heartbeat and Elder's prayers.
My mind was tranquil and my heart vibrant as my spirit braided
into the energies of the women who came before me
and those who are coming.
Birth, Growth, Death, Transformation.
The circle continues to unfold.

Women are sacred.
Women are resilient.
Women are transformational beings.

HEAR OUR VOICES
HEAR OUR HEARTS.

Stories of Transformation

I never ever thought I would be saying this about jail, but you know I'm so glad I got what I'm doing, time wise, that is. Why? Because I would never have got so strong about my feelings and never met the wonderful women that were in the same shoes I was.

—Anonymous

Paragraphs of Passion

W

I would love to work with addicts who lost their children in the system or with children who lost their parents in addiction or with children in foster care who later reach the criminal system.

X

My passion is positive thinking and the self-conscious mind. I have learned so much about how deeply we are connected to our unconsciousness.

Y

My passion is to make a difference in people's lives. When I'm talking to the people about my disease, it hits them right where I want it to. Then, afterwards, when you have teenagers writing you letters, telling you what they are going through, then I know what my passion is.

Z

I believe to every negative there is a positive. At times you just have to dig deep to find it.

A

My passion is spirituality because it improves a person's physical, mental, and emotional state.

B

My passion is my son. I want to learn to be a better parent to better my son's life as well as mine.

C

My dream is to go to central America and work in an orphanage.

Doctor's Journey

RUTH ELWOOD MARTIN

WOMEN ARE WRITING NAMES *on the wall opposite the gym, names of women who have died inside prison or outside, following their release. I recognize former patients among the names. There are too many names on the wall for me to be able to count them all. Every woman on the wall was someone's daughter, sister, mother, friend.*

Here, at this time, in this prison, women writing names on the wall are remembering and mourning other women's passing. Here, they are feeling grief. Other memories may surface, violence, death, loss, senseless, perpetual tragedies, year after year, generation after generation.

As a family physician, I yearn for people to be healthy. What does "health" and "healing" mean for women in prison? For women who have experienced trauma, endured multiple adverse childhood events, and lived with drug use, violence, losses, and crime, what is health? And, how can they possibly attain health, against so many obstacles?

—Journal entry

The World Health Organization (WHO) has stated that:

> Concepts of mental health include subjective wellbeing, perceived self-efficacy, autonomy, competence, intergenerational dependence and recognition of the ability to realize one's intellectual and emotional potential. It has also been defined as a state of wellbeing whereby individuals recognize their abilities, are able to cope with the normal stresses of life, work productively and fruitfully, and make a contribution to their communities. (7)

These concepts of mental health encompass two dimensions: functioning and feelings. Positive feelings include subjective well-being, life satisfaction and happiness. Positive functioning includes engagement, fulfilment, sense of meaning and social well-being. (Huppert; Lyubomirsky, King and Diener; Samman; Ryan and Deci).

Mental health and well-being are fundamental elements of resilience, health assets, capabilities, and positive adaptation, which enable women to cope, to flourish and to experience good health and social outcomes (Friedli 38). Population health studies demonstrate that positive mental health and well-being bring significant benefits for health and quality of life, for individuals and for their communities (Luszczynska, Benight and Cieslak; Harris and Barraclough; Keyes; Steptoe, Gibson, Hamer, and Wardle).

I have observed, over my years inside a women's prison, that hope tips the balance of a woman's life. Imagine life as a teeter-totter with *belief in change* at the pivot. As hope grows and swells, the teeter-totter balance of life shifts—emotionally, spiritually, mentally and physically—and an inner-self emerges with, "I think I can do it!"

This prison gave incarcerated women the opportunity to be passionate; to feel joy, laughter, fear, anger, and grief; to be curious and to try; to succeed and to fail; to believe and to have faith. In addition, this prison gave incarcerated women the opportunity to develop relationships with people who believed in them and who affirmed them with, "*I know that you can do it.*"

Some women tell us that the presence of babies in prison turned their lives around. Other women tell us that their emerging faith or spirituality inside prompted them to change. For others, the passion of doing meaningful work in prison opened their eyes. Other women tell us that having fun, for the first time in their lives, made them realize that they could live without drugs. Most women will say the fact that someone in prison *believed* in them for the first time, belief that they *could* do it, had a profound impact. This gave them hope that change was possible.

In this final chapter, you will read some women's stories of healing and transformation that occurred because they spent time in prison—*this* prison—at *this* point in their lives. In addition, you will read some reflections about what makes a "successful" prison.

REFERENCES

Friedli, L. *Mental Health, Resilience and Inequalities.* Geneva: WHO Regional Office for Europe, 2009.

Harris, E. C. and B. Barraclough. "Excess Mortality of Mental Disorder." *The British Journal of Psychiatry* 173 (1998): 11-53.

Huppert, F. A., N. Baylis, and B. Keverne, eds. *The Science of Wellbeing.* Oxford: Oxford University Press, 2005.

Keyes, C. L. M. "The Nexus of Cardiovascular Disease and Depression Revisited: The Complete Mental Health Perspective and the Moderating Role of Age and Gender." *Aging & Mental Health* 8 (3) (2004): 266-274.

Luszczynska, A., C. Benight, and R. Cieslak. "Self-efficacy and Health-Related Outcomes of Collective Trauma: A Systematic Review." *European Psychologist* 14 (1) (2009): 51-62.

Lyubomirsky S., L. King, and E. Diener. "The Benefits of Frequent Positive Affect: Does Happiness Lead to Success?" *Psychological Bulletin* 131 (6) (2005): 803-855.

Samman E. *Psychological and Subjective Wellbeing: A Proposal for Internationally Comparable Indicators.* Oxford: Oxford Poverty and Human Development Initiative (OPHI), 2007.

Steptoe, A., E. L. Gibson, M. Hamer, and J. Wardle. "Neuroendocrine and Cardiovascular Correlates of Positive Affect Measured by Ecological Momentary Assessment and by Questionnaire." *Psychoneuroendocrinology* 32 (2007): 56–64.

World Health Organization (WHO). "Declaration on Prison Health as Part of Public Health." Moscow: WHO, 2003. Web.

Time of Hope

MO KORCHINSKI

The end, it's just the beginning
One's spirit lost and held hostage with aching,
Tears of fear, now tears of joy
Building sky scrapers one soul at a time
Up
Up
High above the fluffy white clouds
The razor sharp fence hell allowed
After mass lingering bright with time
Stopped beating the beat of one's drum
Lost the hope but now it's found
Ways to cope,
Angels of life,
Timeless adversities
Tip of the iceberg in the blue deep sea
Slowly melting, from the dark dark past
One drop at a time
Drip
Drip
Drip
Puddling in a pool of crystal clear light
Reaching out to the hand that might
Chatting on Facebook
Or meeting with one
Helping to beat the cycle of crime
Once for dope but now there's hope

Dreams

MO KORCHINSKI

It was late that night of nights
So very late that night of nights
When something scary caused a scare
When something hairy raised my hair
Dreams of being under this horrible curse
Dreams of dying from inside out
At night always deadens this fear
How I hate to dream at night
So very late at night of nights
A gift of a dream catcher from my Elder
To hang in my window above my bed
Like a spider web ready to catch its prey
Circular in shape with a hole in the centre
Words from the wise dreams are visions
Messages from the spirit world
To guide and to protect
So very late at night of nights
Good dreams pass through the centre of the web
Remembering only the good dreams
Bad dreams are caught
Stuck in the web
Burnt away with the first ray of light

Being in a prison for nine months raised my level of what's acceptable and what isn't—my bottom—without me even knowing it. Gradually, I knew that things wouldn't get any better if I kept picking up dope. Gradually, I knew that I was done with this life. I wish I could explain "why?" or "when?" or "exactly how?" but I can't muddle out the reasons for that magic "done" button. I just knew that I was done.

— Joy Happyheart

The Little Prison that Could

JOY HAPPYHEART

ICOULD TELL A LOT OF OTHER STORIES that I consider mine, but won't as this is the place to tell my story of what happened for me in ACCW—the Little Prison that Could.

Everything changed when I was sentenced for trafficking to ACCW for nine months, which was the longest time I had been inside. Things changed during that time. My head started to clear out. I maybe smoked a little weed or speed once in a while during that time, but I wasn't doing the hard drugs. I started to feel decent in my body again. I started to function—thinking and feeling—without the drugs. I had stuff to do. I began to heal. I even reached out and reconnected with my family. That reconnection gave hope.

We had to show up for work each day; we could not lie around in bed all day. It was a "step up" for me; a "step up" in my working and my relating. Horticulture was a good fit for me. I am a busy person and had some gardening skill—I grew pot in the past. I would go on tangents— once I was figuring out how to get rid of mites and it would almost become an obsession. It was something to focus on other than dope.

After nine months, I got out on probation to a recovery house, but relapsed horribly for three weeks. I overdosed on heroin and pissed my pants in the Downtown Eastside. I woke up in St. Paul's Hospital, with my pissed pants and only one shoe. I was sent from hospital to a shelter and I said to them, "Send me to a recovery house. I am willing to play by the rules now." The recovery house was a terrible place; the rules were arbitrary, it didn't feel safe, as if I might relapse. I didn't want to be there.

When my breaches for my relapse came up, I asked my parole officer and the courts if they could send me back to ACCW. I knew I would be safer and happier in prison than I was in this recovery house. Prison felt like home, I wasn't safe on the streets, I wasn't safe in what I knew of recovery, but I did feel safe in ACCW during those times. They sent me back for a few months.

When I got out, I moved to the Valley and life's been amazing since. I am half way through a Bachelor's in Social Work with a 3.73 GPA. I have a full-time job, and I'm driving around in my little truck that I paid for myself. I have a credit card and pay bills.

A softness came over everyone in the prison. We all changed at least a little because of those babies. I began drumming with the Elder Holy Cow, and working on my spirit again. My time went by pretty quickly at ACCW, probably because they kept us so busy. We had corn roasts and hamburger sales. We had sports days and slip and slide and karaoke. And we had the most amazing recreation therapist, Alison Granger-Brown, who helped us in every way humanly possible. It didn't matter what she had to do; she made sure women left with clean clothes and a good spirit.

—Amber Christie

The Prison that Changed My Life

AMBER CHRISTIE

WHEN I THINK ABOUT WHAT CHANGED in my life in 2005, I know for sure that it was the correctional institution I was held in. I'd been in Surrey Pretrial and Burnaby Correctional Centre for Women so many times I lost count.

Following my arrest, I was transferred to Surrey Pretrial, where I was told I could go to a place called ACCW. I was very excited because I knew that I would be able to talk to other people instead of being segregated for 23 hours a day. Though I tried my best to hide it, I was drug sick. My best attempts failed. On the trip from Surrey to Alouette, I was sick all over the van.

When I arrived at ACCW, I was sent to health care where I was checked and then sent to a unit. I couldn't believe the place I'd been sent to. I'd never seen anything like it. The closest I had seen to an open space was the track at BCCW.

I was sent to my unit and given a huge black duffel bag with clothes and all my bedding for the next six months. The following days were quite different from any of the other stays I'd had in other institutions. I was sent to work in a horticulture job. I was still very sick and I struggled with the work. I spoke with an officer and she told me that she would try to get me a job doing unit maintenance.

In the meantime, I was sent to see the doctor because I was very sick—not only from the drug withdrawal but from ten years of living on Hastings Street. I had acquired unforgiving illnesses that needed medical intervention. This is where I met Ruth (Dr. Martin). She was the kindest physician I had seen in many years. She listened to me and explained my illnesses to me. Then she explained all my treatment options. There weren't many. I had to stay clean or I was going to die—it was as simple as that. She encouraged me on a weekly basis to reconnect with my family, and after a few weeks, I did. I hadn't spoken with my family in close to eight years so there were some bridges to mend.

My family came to visit me on a weekly basis for the next six months. I was starting to feel better, and after ten years, I was finally thinking that I needed to do something different with my life. I began drumming with Holy Cow, and working on my spirit again.

That prison made me remember who I was before I went to the streets, and today I am eternally grateful, and so is my family. I have a life today that is so worth living. I've been off the streets and out of prison and off drugs for almost five years now. I have a beautiful son and fiancé who are my life, and I am pregnant with my next child. I have a job that I love, a job that was only made possible by the passions of imprisoned women. Our voices were only heard because we had a warden who believed that, with the right circumstances, we were all capable and worthy of redemption and change. It's amazing how a little bit of kindness can change a life.

I work with women from provincial prisons every day. I see every day the failures in the justice system: the lack of housing resources and lack of community in the prison; the programs that have been cut; and all of the sad reminders that "the prison that changed my life" is no longer the same. I can only hope that through our voices, someone again hears that things need to change.

Three Prayers of Thanks

JEN FLAVEL

I AM ONLY 26 YEARS OLD NOW, but I've already lived a long, full life. I've been down more roads, conquered more obstacles, and survived more painful scenarios than anyone at my age should have to. I thank God every single day for handing me the life He did because eventually I learned that He never dishes out more than I could handle. Not once did He leave me on my own while I struggled; even if I couldn't see Him or refused to acknowledge Him, I now know He was always there.

I realize now that what was keeping me on the street wasn't other people. It wasn't because God forgot about me and took joy in my personal pain. I was out there for so long because I was looking for answers to questions that I already had the answers to. I just didn't know it, and even after it was pointed out to me, I didn't know how to access this knowledge. I was angry, hurt, and confused. I just wanted it all to go away; I just wanted some sanity, some justification, and some peace. But even when it was right in front of me, I couldn't accept it. Yet, I always held on to a hope for a better tomorrow. When I was hungry, I still shared my bread, and when I was freezing in the middle of the night, I would still cuddle and try to share what little warmth I had. When I was hurt and degraded I thought 'ha, like that is anything new.' I just wanted to love and to be loved and I wanted someday to look back at the life I was living and think 'wow, am I glad that's all over.' I wanted to feel whole and I wanted to belong somewhere. Not in city parks, or alley ways, or shacks; I wanted to find a home. I wanted to be able to close my eyes and feel home, not like I was falling.

Prison saved my life. Prison and all the programs that I idled through, thinking that it was just a way to get a good log for the day. I rediscovered the sober and real me. Slowly, very, very slowly, the streets, the drugs, the reputations, the memories, and ideas of who I thought I was, started to melt away and change. Eventually, I started to realize that being a drug addict, working girl, hustler, and a scam artist, were all bad choices that I made. I started to realize that they were just bad choices and that they didn't define who I was. I wasn't all of those things; they were things that I had done. It took time to come to terms with this and accept that it was true. After accepting that, I was taught how to look at the way I thought about my life. This led me to the awakening that changed my life. Simply by realizing that I am a beautiful soul embodied by a beautiful face, living and experiencing life just as I am supposed to. And I am forever grateful that God finally allowed me to wake up and see myself through His eyes for the first time in my life.

Each day I say three prayers of thanks, and at least two prayers for strength and patience. I say a final prayer every night just to remind myself that superheroes do regain their powers. Mother Goose does remember her rhymes and those dirty dogs are just those puppies that you always hear about getting kicked, but you never see it happen. Everybody has a story, everything does happen for a reason, and when and if I'm ever seeking out answers, I pray. Then I listen.

Proud of Who I Am Today

ANNETTE DUBRULE

I HAVE MADE SOME MAJOR MISTAKES, but I am back on my feet and on the path to change. I am ready to better my life. When I was addicted, a friend used to tell me, "Annette, smarten up, you're better than this! What's wrong with you? See that door? Do not fear the door! Those who fear the door will never know the difference but those who choose to open the door will be the difference! Open the door and walk through and don't look back!" I used to think he was nuts and wondered what door he was talking about. Today I know what he meant. What lies on the other side of the door is freedom.

Soon I will be three years clean and criminally free. I am making progress in changing the rest of my life. I am finally taking that huge step of reaching out and admitting to others that I need help, and not just to my friends and family who know me and put up with me, but to others who are going to help me overcome my issues and help me learn what it is I need to do to better and further myself.

I'm still embarrassed about my past and will always be. I'm not proud of my mistakes. I am, however, proud of who I am today and I do realize my past is a part of who I am.

Hope Comes Before Fear

ROSIE JONES

I AM HOPING I CAN BE STRONG and stay strong as I face the fear that's coming. I begin treatment soon. Not enforced, I'm doing it for me. The fear is getting stronger each day, but I know hope comes before fear. There are three doors in jail: the first door is my bedroom door, the second door is gate one, the third door is gate two, and to get through those doors I have to take one step at a time. I know it's going to be very slippery.

I pray for all the women who wrote me a letter and even the ones who didn't write me. I hope the best for you all. It took me twenty years in and out of jail to finally say that's it. This is no jail talk. As I close the life I had and leave it behind, I wish you all luck in your future, my sisters.

Jessica's Story[1]

HAVE YOU EVER HAD TO LOOK innocent people in the eye after you've defrauded them? This was my first time. I've always been able to hide behind their ID until I got caught passing off someone's licence to get a loaner car. It wound up being the guy's girlfriend's ID. He said "Do you know how this feels?" I now know this, and I felt disgusted with myself—seeing my pathetic reflection, in the rear view mirror staring back at me in the back of the police car. The man was in tears. What could I say to make him feel better? "I'm sorry?" How many times have I said sorry in my life? I knew whatever I said to him, he wouldn't believe me because I'm an addict and a con.

Being faced with the people I hurt in life gave me a wakeup call. I never before had to see the pain that I put in other people's lives. I didn't ever really care, but faced with no way out, I saw the destruction my behaviours caused and I'm not proud. The image of myself hanging my head down brought me to tears. How could I let myself get so out of control for eight years? How do I get my life back? But in reality how do others get back theirs after I have stolen them?

I have since then completely quit. No little thing here on the side or a little bit there. I'm done.

---

[1]This story is reprinted from *Women in2 Healing Newsletter* 2 (September 2008): 7. Available at www.womenin2healing.org/newsletters.

The Big Turnaround

MO KORCHINSKI

I SPENT TEN MONTHS ON REMAND, and during this time I turned forty years old. Wow, forty! I was so sick of my life on the outside that I didn't want to leave jail. On the outside, I had nothing in my life: no hope, no family, no home, and no one who cared. I had nothing. In jail I had a job, purpose, support, friends, and people who cared. I didn't know how to function in society, to learn how to become a productive member of society. So many people inside the jail cared and believed in me. That was something new for me. So I put my name on the list to go to a local treatment centre, but I couldn't get funding as I was on remand.

The fear of thinking that I could be let out of jail from court with the clothes on my back, no money, right back in my war zone was overwhelming. I knew that I couldn't do it again, go through all the anxiety, the rollercoaster from hell. I was on the waiting list for treatment for three months. Then I was granted one month of funding to get into treatment and into court to get bail. I could have gone to court and got time served, but I knew if I did, I might not make it back this time. I guess this helped me fight for what I wanted even when at the beginning I wasn't too sure if I did want to go to treatment.

When the day came for me to leave, I was right back to not wanting to leave. The staff kept calling me to records, but I figured if I didn't hear them, then they might forget me. Well, the girls found me and were all waiting to drum me out and sing for me. As I walked through the gates, three bald eagles flew above me.

My Elder taught me that the bald eagle is the Grandfathers watching over me, and I knew when I saw them that I was being watched and looked out for. This gave me the strength to move forward and leave the walls of the prison, hopefully for the last time. I went for treatment in Maple Ridge so I could still be close to the support that I had found in jail. When I got to the treatment centre it took me a half hour to get the nerve to walk inside the doors. The fear of something new, of not knowing what was ahead of me, was overwhelming.

The biggest reason I'm doing well is the support I've received from women who have been in jail and are now on the outside of the fence. I've learned to take baby steps in my new life and keep telling myself over and over that I will get through. I must just breathe. When I look back, I know my life has been hard, but I am looking ahead now. I am hopeful for new stories.

When people living with HIV/AIDS or those at high risk for infection (as they are in prison), change their behaviour, learn new skills, and make a commitment to the improvement of their health, there are fewer new infections and a decrease in health-care access inside and outside of prison. These benefits, as well as a reduction in recidivism as people heal, are worth all our efforts to encourage prison officials to continue to move away from penitentiary-style incarceration, and toward restorative- style prisons where people are given the opportunity to improve their circumstances and not simply be warehoused in punishment.

—Terry Howard

Grey Day Reflections

RUTH ELWOOD MARTIN

BRENDA TOLE, ALISON GRANGER-BROWN, and Ruth Elwood Martin met for a day, in November 2011, a grey day on the Gulf Islands. Lynn Fels bore witness to our conversations. We met to reflect and to write, and to summarize what we had learned. We wanted to be able to contribute to this book, moving forward as we reflected on, "What did we learn?" and, "What implications are here for others who are thinking of doing similar things?"

Paper and pens poised for writing, with coffee at hand, we began talking. It was three years since management changes and Brenda and Alison's departure from ACCW; we were ready to reflect, together, and to revisit past events. We talked and talked, and talked some more, and we did not pick up our pens. An audio recorder, nestled amongst the cheese, fruit, and coffee mugs on the table, captured our conversation, which Ruth listened to later as she wrote this section.

Trust

Brenda said that wardens of women's institutions have opportunities for introducing innovation. Because the women's population in any province is small and unique, a women's warden can propose to her/ his peers (that is, wardens of the male institutions) and to her/his boss (that is, the ministry headquarters): "I think this would work well, and I would like to try this." Brenda says that you need trust with your boss to be able to do this; similarly, your boss needs to be able to trust your judgement. You need to have his/her trust in order to have the flexibility to be able to implement women-centred approaches, which will be unique to women's institutions and are different than those necessitated for all of the men's institutions. For Brenda, the trust was there at the beginning of her tenure. At the end of her tenure, changed personnel resulted in a loss of trust.

Listen to Ideas

Brenda listened to ideas for improvement from the incarcerated women themselves, from the prison staff and from people in the outside community (e.g. Sarah Payne, the nurse leader of Fir Square, BC Women's Hospital). In addition, several community organizations were very keen to help and they were able to share their expertise and ideas about community involvement. These community organizations saw incarcerated women as part of their mandate, and therefore they were happy to invest in women inside the centre.

Employ Staff Who Make Things Happen

Within the institution, Brenda employed staff who would seek to make things happen, rather than staff who looked for reasons why things would not work. Alison explained that when you arrived at ACCW in the morning, you felt the positive energy as you entered the gates, "Women can heal, women can get healthy, and there is hope." The energy is about wanting to work together to bring improvement, and that there is hope.

Involve Everyone

How can you move systems and people who are set in their ways? Brenda used the analogy, "It's like turning a tanker." You have to spend time, lots of time, listening to peoples' concerns and fears. Brenda used to think that one could implement change with the following sequence, "This idea makes sense, this idea is logical. I am going to give staff the information and then I will implement this idea." But, this sequence does not work. Staff need to be involved in the process. Staff need time to see it, to sense it, and to express their concerns and fears. As the leader, you keep your eyes focused on where you are going, and you keep moving everyone there; have meetings, listen to them, support them, be persistent, but keep moving towards where you want to be.

Brenda remembered that when she initially worked with the BC Ministry of Children and Family Development (MCFD), regarding creating a mother-baby program inside ACCW, the MCFD staff presented so many barriers for women having their babies inside a correctional institution. Brenda engaged them in a process and after two years she was amazed to see how much they had changed. In addition, incarcerated women who previously had very little trust in authority organizations (e.g. social workers) gradually started to voluntarily approach social workers (who were visiting ACCW because of the mother baby program), to ask for their help in finding their children, rather than seeing social workers as a negative thing in their lives.

Be Transparent

One principle that Brenda tried to adhere to was, "transparency of information." When you are in a position of power, you can withhold information with an attitude of, "They do not need to know this information." Brenda found that people respond to information because they can then understand why decisions are made. This engages people in the decision-making processes. Alison says that women can then be innovative and creative in working out the situations they find themselves in, such as dealing with limited supplies and resources. For example, supplies for the Halloween party were limited, so women used whatever was around such as toilet paper and sanitary pads.

Normalize Health for the Whole Prison

One of the problems in prison is that 'health care' becomes medicalized. The nurses, who work in the medical clinic, become the gate keepers though which women have to push in order to see a physician. The physician parachutes in and out of the medical clinic, sees patients one-on-one, and writes prescriptions as a panacea for all ill health.

During this time at ACCW (2004-2007), health became more normalized and less medicalized. Nurses and physicians spent more time in the prison environment, outside the confines of the medical clinic. For example, nurses began to visit each living unit, engaging with women in conversations around health. Incarcerated women would approach nurses to ask for their assistance in finding information on health conditions and health prevention. Ruth would spend time outside of the medical clinic, in the research room, in the gym and in operational meetings with wardens and correctional staff, which became group meetings about health, illness, and prevention. The physician's role expanded to became one of interpretation, knowledge translation, and information sharing. In addition, the engagement of the Aboriginal Elder, the Aboriginal women and the Aboriginal educators in this process, facilitated a shift of focus away from, "How do we access health care?" to, "How do we become healthy in all spheres of health—physical, mental, emotional and spiritual?"

Respect: The Essential Leadership Quality

Respect is key. Respect overrides everything you do. Respect normalizes everything you do. When you treat people with respect (in a power imbalance) you get a different response. Women who are seen as behaviourally different have become that way by torture, because isolation and segregation is a form of torture. *You reap what you sow.* If you treat incarcerated women, staff and contractors in a manner that is not respectful, you will create people who do not behave normally. If you treat people with respect, they will help with solving the problems when things go sideways, even though you may have differences of opinion.

When you have a leader (warden) who is respectful, staff feel safer, supported, heard. A leader should be visionary, creative, democratic and approachable. He/she should be able to listen to ideas, and to create a space for people to do what they do best, making it safer for people to do what they do. People do what they do best with good communication. A leader who micromanages and is controlling creates an unsafe environment.

A warden can apply the same principle—respect—for incarcerated women as for the staff. The expectation is that incarcerated women will take an active role in moving ideas forward; the women will generate an environment that is safer for themselves and for the staff. Nothing is ever perfect; people make mistakes. When a mistake in choice of action or an error in judgement happens, you approach the situation and individuals involved with, "How are we going to make this not happen in the future? What can you say about it? What can you learn from it?" The expectation and responsibility of everyone involved is that we will create a respective and supportive environment to work and learn together. We have expectations that you are treated with respect, that we expect you to do well and that you can take responsibility to move things forward. When things go sideways, we address it. We don't develop policy that is based on "what if" scenarios and the "potential of risk."

Maximize Women's Relationships with Children and Families in Everything

For most incarcerated women, the most significant concerns and biggest potential influence on women's health are pregnancy, children, and family relationships. This focus and concern is supported by published evidence in medical and social sciences regarding attachment theory. Therefore, let us maximise how we engage these issues to make a difference, to give women hope to create change. Every aspect of everything we do inside a correctional institution could foreseeably relate to existing and consequent relationships with women's children, partners, and family of origin. For example, we could maximise incarcerated women's contact with children and families (using a variety of communication venues and face-to-face visiting), and we could maximise the impact of education and self-development skills related to interpersonal, emotional and parenting skills. Brenda notes that the "success" for the women who were engaged in the mother-baby program (if you equate success with low recidivism rates) was better than for any of the other prison programs for women.

Provide Therapeutic Warmth

Much of current correctional practice is based upon the principle of the withdrawal of "therapeutic warmth" (Bordin, 1994; Ross, Polaschek, and Ward, 2008): that is, withdrawing therapeutic warmth will correct a person's bad behaviour. The narratives of prison life as portrayed in *Arresting Hope* illustrate that this principle is a myth.

Babies living with their mothers during their incarceration at ACCW (2005-2007) seemed such a "normal" thing to be happening inside our prison gates. Tragically, in 2008, a new management direction discontinued the ACCW Mother-Baby Unit, such that, following their delivery in hospital, women returned to prison without their babies.[1] One incarcerated woman, whose baby was apprehended at birth in 2008, said from her prison cell, while pumping breast milk to give to the foster parents, "Crying over spilt milk takes on a new meaning."

We echo Justice Louise Arbour, who wrote in 1996:

> The administration of criminal justice does not end with the verdict and the imposition of a sentence.... Ill-adapted correctional policies borrowed from models designed for men, have failed to produce the substantive equality to which women offenders are entitled.... The chances of success for a progressive correctional experiment are highest in women's corrections. (Arbour, 1996, p. 13)

Arresting Hope bears witness to the benefit of providing therapeutic warmth for incarcerated women.

[1]In December 2013, BC Supreme Court Justice Carol Ross ruled that the right of a mother and baby to be together is protected by Section 7 of the Canadian Charter of Rights and Freedoms: imprisoned mothers have the constitutional right to care for their newborn babies. In June,

2014, Alouette Correctional Centre for Women re-opened a Mother-Baby Unit.

REFERENCES

Arbour, L. "Commission of Inquiry into Certain Events at the Prison for Women in Kingston." Ottawa: Canada Communication Group Publishing, 1996.

Bordin, E. S. (1994). "Theory and Research on the Therapeutic Working Alliance: New Directions." *The Working Alliance: Theory, Research and Practice*. Ed. A. O. H. L. S. Greenberg. New York: Wiley, 1994. 13-37.

Ross, E. C., D. L. L. Polaschek, and T. Ward. "The Therapeutic Alliance: A Theoretical Revision for Offender Rehabilitation." *Aggression and Violent Behavior* 13 (6) (2008): 462-480.

Welcoming the Stranger Home

LYNN FELS

"YOU'VE GOT A THING FOR THE PROFESSOR, don't you?" One of the inmates asks.

I look at her alarmed, *how did she know?*

The women look up from their writing, watching me speculatively.

"Just kidding you," she says, and we laugh, but I know that she knows that she's caught me out.

Working with the women on the prison research team has kept me on my toes, attentive, acutely aware of how little I know about heart-ache and abuse, about broken families, about life on the street, about life inside the gates.

"What does 'cracking the gate' mean? Who are the blueshirts?" I ask, as we transcribe our research notes (Meyer and Fels): Prison inmates teaching university researchers as we work and learn together.

Women marked as criminals are someone's sister, mother, aunt, daughter, niece, granddaughter, or grandmother. When we stop to listen to their stories, or when we invite them to engage with us in research or to organize communal activities; or when they are given the opportunity to be responsible for their own well-being and, perhaps more importantly, to become responsible for the well-being of their fellow inmates, we are asking them, and ourselves, to imagine a correctional system that attends to the stories, the hopes, the fears, the grief, the loss, the desires that each of us embody, inside and outside the gates.

When engaging is a shared project of renewal, strangers become individual women seeking release from the narratives and expectations of their lived experiences; their stories invite us to create conditions within and outside the prison gates so that something new might come into being. In turn, they offer ideas, suggestions, and insights into the complex conditions, relationships, and experiences that have brought them to where they are. In dialogue, they illuminate the challenges, barriers, and complicities imposed by society, as they have experienced within their individual communities, as they seek to find their way to meaningful employment and healthy relationships and lives.

Hannah Arendt, a philosopher and refugee from Germany during the Second World War, spent her life questioning how ordinary men (and women) could do evil things, and in her wondering, conceived the concept of natality. With each child's birth, the child arrives in a world of colliding narratives. We ask: Who is present to welcome this child's arrival? Who is absent? What are our responsibilities? What opportunities do we offer this child? Details of birth, heritage, geographic, educational, social, political, economic, parental realities situate the newborn in relationship to all those who come into the child's presence. Arendt (1958) invited us to ask ourselves, *Who am I?* and *Who will I become in the presence of and in relationship with this child?* How we choose to welcome each other and how we learn to navigate the journey together matters.

Understanding natality becomes more difficult when we seek to understand our responsibilities in terms of the arrival of those living in or leaving our nation's federal and provincial prisons: women marked by stories of abuse, crime, grief, loss; women who habitually cycle and recycle through correctional institutions in search of home, employment, love. How do we, as individuals, as health and social workers, as educators, as community members, greet those with criminal records who come into our midst? *Who do we become in their presence? What actions do we choose? And why?*

An individual, recently incarnated, announces her vulnerability, her newness; yet she also arrives within an ongoing narrative that already anticipates her future; she arrives in a state of "belatedness" (Levison) burdened with the expectations of future deeds (they'll head straight back to the streets, they'll return to what they've known). Might we silence our expectations, our perceptions, those time-worn narratives that hold us fast, so that we may listen to their stories, find courage to enter into dialogue, and together explore new solutions, new possibilities of engagement?

The stories of incarcerated women are heartbreaking; they live within the trauma of life experience. As witnesses, we are called to engage in a reciprocity of responsibility. Even as we ask, *who are you?*, we, in turn, must ask, *who am I?* We discover that we must learn to offer hospitality, as philosopher Derrida encouraged, not knowing how, or who will open their hearts to us.

> Pure and unconditional hospitality, hospitality itself, opens or is in advance open to someone who is neither expected nor invited, to whomever arrives as an absolutely foreign visitor, as a new arrival, nonindentifiable and unforeseeable, in short, wholly, other. (cited in Borradori 128-129)

What has been our experience working with the women inmates of the correctional centre? While there have been challenges, stumbles, and setbacks, we've experienced wonderful moments of success. Learning together has been key to understanding the possibilities of reimagining how we might engage with those who come into our prisons and those who leave. And we have become aware of the responsibilities and unique opportunities that arise from such engagement. To recognize and respond to a situation is to bring to it a sense of judgement, a willingness to engage, with acute awareness of one's own social, political, cultural, environmental narratives and biases, attending to relationality, integrity, compassion and reciprocal responsibility. We learn that we need to nurture what has become an exciting space of possibility. Our task, as Natasha Levison reminds us, "is to preserve natality, therefore insuring that the gap between past and future remains a space of freedom and possibility" (30). Like a child's tug on the sleeve, natality calls us to be present to *this moment, here, now.*

This shared journey of prison doctor, warden, recreational therapist, and women inmates may be understood as a gift of natality, one of great risk, one of great responsibility—a calling for mutual respect and reciprocity. Held within the concept of natality is mutual vulnerability, shared opportunities for freedom from predictable narratives, release of a tethered imagination (Greene 1995). Yet, here, too, within these moments of encounter is complicity and deep shame for what has been left undone in the past, what is unfolding in a difficult present. So often, we are in the presence of women who have found themselves in situations of crime that come on the heels of what should have been done, but was not, prior to the first wounding. As Arendt reminded us,

> Basically, we are always educating for a world that is or is becoming out of joint.... The problem is simply to educate in such a way that a setting right remains actually possible, even though it can, of course, never be assured. (1961: 189)

It is through education that Arendt proposed that we might come to new beginnings and thoughtful action. To reimagine the gap between past and future is our pedagogical and communal challenge as we consider the conditions of our prisons, the experiences of the women who are caught in the cycle of crime, and how we individually and communally respond to each other both inside and outside the gates. Ultimately, Arendt placed her hope and faith in the children that we invite to engage in the world's renewal:

> And education, too, is where we decide whether we love our children enough not to expel them from our world and leave them to their own devices, nor to strike from their hands their chance of undertaking something new, something unforeseen by us, but to prepare them in advance for the task of renewing a common world. (1961: 196)

Reading this quote, we could just as easily replace the word "children" with "prisoner." In society's response to those who populate our prisons, particularly in current political times, we too often withhold the funding, opportunity, and permission from those we imprison to engage anew.

To invite women in prison to reimagine their lives through creative and meaningful action is to offer each woman inmate a lifetime of possibility, a narrative of renewal. The world in which we dwell is a socially, politically, economically, environmentally, culturally, communally constructed reality. Understanding that we come to our relationships within systems already scripted is the first step towards questioning why we engage in the actions that we do.

Maxine Greene (1978), advised that we be wide-awake, to seek to learn who we *are*, to be mindfully aware of our moral positioning, so that we might attend with integrity and care and imagination, those who come amongst us. Each individual has something precious to offer. Awareness of our stories, and how we came to be where we are helps us begin to participate as active responsible individuals. As bell hooks reminded us, quoting writer, Jane Ellen Wilson:

> Only by coming to terms with my own past, my own background, and seeing that in the context of the world at large, have I begun to find my true voice and to understand that, since it is my own voice, that no pre-cut niche exists for it; that part of the work to be done is making a place, with others, where my and our voices can stand clear of the background noise and voice our concerns as part of a larger song. (177)

It is our presence, the unique song that we sing, solo and in the company of others that matters in the moment of each new encounter; for in receiving newness, we behold and hold a place of renewal, restoration (Lange), and possibility for ourselves and for those who come to sing within our presence.

To be wide-awake is to recognize the possibilities that are in the moment of each individual's presence, in each encounter; to listen deeply to the echoes of what has been lost, the stories untold, and those songs yet a heartbeat away, and know that we are meeting this individual *as if for the very first time*. It is to remember that our responsibility is to receive each individual with grace, with forgiveness, with wide-awakeness of the gifts they offer. All of us stand at the threshold that invites new possible beginnings. It is only now, in listening to the women's stories, in sharing in the pain, the laughter, the grief, the joy, in our experience of creating *something new*, that we may understand the journey that we have travelled, side by side.

And so, we come now to this moment of encounter and invitation: a woman enters or exits a prison, in your presence, in our midst. Who will we choose to become in the presence of each other?

Special acknowledgement to Dr. Karen Meyer whose writing and conversations are woven through this writing (see Meyer and Fels; Fels, Meyer and Martin).

REFERENCES

Arendt, H. *The Human Condition.* Chicago: University of Chicago Press, 1958.

Arendt, H. "The Crisis in Education." *In Between Past and Future: Six Exercises of Political Thought.* New York: The Viking Press, 1961. 170-193.

Borradori, G. *Philosophy in a Time of Terror: Dialogues with Jurgen Habermas and Jacques Derrida.* Chicago: University of Chicago Press, 2003.

Fels, L., K. Meyer, and R. Elwood Martin. "Words Within Prison Gates: Participatory Action Research as an Action of Restorative Justice." *International Perspectives on Restorative Justice in Education.* Ed. J. Charlton, S. Pavelka and P. J. Verrecchia. Kanata, ON: J. Charlton Publishing Ltd., 2011. 69-88.

Green, M. *Releasing the Imagination: Essays on Education, the Arts, and Social Change.* San Francisco: Jossey-Bass Publishers, 1995.

Greene, M. *Landscapes of Learning.* New York: Teachers College Press, 1978.

hooks, b. *Teaching to Transgress.* New York: Routledge, 1994.

Lange, E. "Transformative and Restorative Learning: A Vital Dialectic for Sustainable Societies." *Adult Education Quarterly* 54 (2004): 121-139.

Levison, N. "The Paradox of Natality: Teaching in the Midst of Belatedness." *Hannah Arendt and Education: Renewing Our Common World.* Ed. M. Gordon. Colorado: Westview, 2001. 37-66.

Meyer, K. and L. Fels. "Breaking Out: Learning Research from 'The Women in Prison Project'." *International Review of Qualitative Research* 2 (2) (2009): 269-290.

What Makes a Successful Prison?[1]

CARL LEGGO

life
ritual
healing
purpose
friendships
reaching out
peer teaching
meaningful work
contributing to others
educational opportunities
making a difference in someone else's life
being involved in the working of the running of the prison
sharing in the responsibility of their environment, activities
a supportive network inside and out the prison gates
reconnecting with my children
non-hierarchial environment
overcoming your demons
reconnecting with family
acceptance from society
hope for a better future
relationship with staff
home upon release
staying drug free
forgiveness
agency
hope

[1]This found poem was created from themes emerging from the conversations, writings and interviews of *Arresting Hope*.

Contributor Notes

EDITOR-AUTHORS

Ruth Elwood Martin
I worked as family physician in Vancouver from 1983 to 2009; I also worked part-time in the medical clinics of BC correctional centres for men and women for seventeen years. I am a Clinical Professor of the School of Population and Public Health, University British Columbia, and an Associate Faculty of the Department of Family Practice. My experiences as a prison physician participatory researcher during the time period of *Arresting Hope* changed me, such that my goal became to foster the improvement of prison health and to engage patients' voices in the process. I helped create the Collaborating Centre for Prison Health and Education, which is a group committed to encouraging and facilitating collaborative opportunities for health, education, research, service and advocacy, to enhance the social well-being and (re)integration of individuals in custody, their families and communities. I also lead the Prison Health Special Interest Focused Practice Group, of the College of Family Physicians of Canada.

Mo Korchinski
Since writing *Arresting Hope,* I have found my three children through Facebook and have a loving relationship with my children today. I am a proud grandmother to a beautiful four-year-old granddaughter, Letisha, who has taught me what unconditional love is. I live independently and am graduated in May 2012 from the Nicola Valley Institute of Technology with my degree in Associate of Arts. I started my Bachelor in Social Work in September 2012. I volunteer as a community-based researcher with Women in2 Healing and work as a research assistant with the Canadian Institute of Health Research

funded project "Doing Time Unlocking the Gates" at the University of British Columbia. I am clean and sober and spend most of my spare time helping others in my community. I feel that the key to turning one's life around and keeping it moving in the right direction is to help others turn their lives around. I co-directed the documentaries *Revolving Door* and *Unlocking the Gates,* which are about women's release from prison, and when the prison gate is unlocked, but the doors to society are kept locked. My passion is to take my experience of addiction and the justice system and show people that changes are needed: to get the voices of women who are still inside of prison heard; and, to get policy-makers to understand that change is needed in the prison system and in the communities.

Lynn Fels

Working on this book project and with those involved in the research project in ACCW has been an unexpected gift for me. I am humbled and awed by the strength, wisdom, and commitment that the women I have met bring to our conversations and shared experiences. I came to understand that the stories we live, dwell in our bodies. We are marked by our beginnings and by those we meet on our life journey, but we may take action to change our narrative. I am a writer and Associate Professor in Arts Education at Simon Fraser University in British Columbia, and a former editor of the on-line education journal, *Educational Insights.* I am passionate about the arts as exploratory spaces for learning. I am currently involved in a five-year research project on arts for social change in Canada. My books include, *Living Together: Unmarried Couples in Canada,* and, co-authored with George Belliveau, *Exploring Curriculum: Performative Inquiry, Role Drama and Learning.*

Carl Leggo

I am a poet and professor in the Department of Language and Literacy Education at the University of British Columbia. I think we can live more joyful lives if we commit ourselves to writing about our lived experiences and sharing our stories, poetry, and wisdom with others. So, it is a joy to work with others to encourage them to write and to reveal their voices with heart and truthfulness. I have published several books of poetry and scholarship, always with a focus on creativity and the arts, including: *Growing Up Perpendicular on the Side of a Hill; View from My Mother's House; Come-By-Chance; Teaching to Wonder: Responding to Poetry in the Secondary Classroom; Lifewriting as Literary Métissage and an Ethos for Our Times* (co-authored with Erika

Hasebe-Ludt and Cynthia Chambers); *Being with A/r/tography* (co-edited with Stephanie Springgay, Rita L. Irwin, and Peter Gouzouasis); *Creative Expression, Creative Education* (co-edited with Robert Kelly); and *Poetic Inquiry: Vibrant Voices in the Social Sciences* (co-edited with Monica Prendergast and Pauline Sameshima).

CONTRIBUTING AUTHORS

Alison Granger-Brown

I was sent quite by accident to the Forensic Psychiatric Hospital for my first practicum in Therapeutic Recreation (TR). Once there I realized that something about the setting was compelling and that I wanted to work in a related field. I completed my preceptorship at Burnaby Correctional Centre for Women and have continued working with incarcerated women ever since. Thirteen years later, I have worked in both provincial and federal custody from segregation to open custody and also with women on parole. The most exciting and fulfilling time of my career was at ACCW. It was an opportunity to start something new as we set a very clear intention from the beginning working together with the women and staff to create a special environment open to creative programming and most especially supporting hope and possibility for us all. I have used my previous education in nursing along with TR and developed my recent academic studies around the learning needs of women in a prison setting. I recently completed my Ph.D. but nothing will equate to what I have learned from the women I have been privileged to journey alongside for the last dozen or so years.

Amber Christie

I am a Cree First Nations woman. I was first incarcerated in 2000 at the age of twenty, and I returned to prison thirty times over the next five years. In my most recent incarceration in 2005, I spent six months inside Alouette Correctional Centre for Women. Before that, I had spent time in Surrey Pretrial and Burnaby Correctional Centre for women. I suffered from a severe heroin addiction for many years and lived on the streets. Today, I have been free of drugs and prisons for five years. I am a mother and a contributing member of society. I am a Research Assistant for the University of British Columbia, working in community-based participatory research. I am employed by the project called "Doing Time," and I am part of the "Women in2 Healing" team. I also work with a community-based participatory research project called "Aboriginal Healing Outside of the Gates." My goal is to support women in the reintegration process so that they can safely reintegrate into their chosen communities.

Brenda Tole

I retired after a thirty-seven-year career with BC Corrections Branch. I graduated with a Bachelor in Education from the University of British Columbia and started my career as a community Probation Officer/Family Court Counsellor. I worked in various communities in the Lower Mainland over the next fifteen years, followed with a variety of management positions in different correctional centres in the custody division. The last position I held was as the Warden of Alouette Correctional Centre for Women from 2003-2007. I live with my husband Mark and spend time with five grown children and six grandchildren between Cultus Lake and Galiano Island.

Christine Hemingway

While incarcerated at ACCW, I was one of many women to start the participatory research program with Dr Ruth Martin. We discovered and learned many things that were needed for women while incarcerated and help for when women are released. I have remained in touch with Women in2 Healing and have helped by telling my story to give women hope that when they are released they are not alone. Since my release in November 2006, I have been very active in trying to help change health care inside the prisons for women. I was also a member of the University of British Columbia roundtable international conference Bonding Through Bars, with many delegates from around the world, to keep mothers and their babies together while incarcerated. My son, who is now twenty years old and an airline pilot, also helped with the roundtable project, voicing his thoughts on how he was affected at the age of eleven years being separated from me for seventeen months. I now own a store and work very hard at communicating with my son, which we didn't do until we both got involved with Bonding Through Bars; it really helped us to open up. My son and I will continue to help mothers connect with their children upon release. I am very grateful that I became involved with the research team and Women in2 healing; it has helped me get my life back and become a productive member of society.

Debra Hanson

I was a passionate member of the ACCW inmate participatory research team. A former restaurant manager, I brought team organizational expertise to the participatory research project. I have two grown daughters who had been in and out of the correctional system and I truly wanted to get involved in helping to build the strengths of the women in the research team. I led the development of an orientation package for all new team members, and the 'paragraphs of passion' exercise, which women participated in when they joined the research team. I taught myself PowerPoint and other computer skills, and then coached other team members in these skills. My research passion was housing, because I knew that housing is the first step to improving women's health when they leave prison. I am currently working as a baker.

Teagen

I have a busy and great life. My son started kindergarten in September 2011 and I'm having a blast helping him with all his school activities. When I'm not with him, I am in class at Douglas College where I am two years into my psychiatric nursing degree. When not at school or with my son, I can be found at the care facility I have been working at since 2008. In our downtime, we love to play outside or visit with our family.

Jen Flavel

Jen was a much loved daughter, mother, and friend to many. She had a passion for photography and took a ton of pictures. Jen's life ended tragically and too early.

Kelly Murphy

While incarcerated in 2005, I participated in the Women In2 Healing research project, which seeks to collaborate with women as they are being released into the community and to improve their health during that process. I have arisen out of abuse and adversity and I am now passionately involved in helping other women find their voice and rise out of oppressive circumstances. Working with narratives and dialogue, I advocate to tell the stories of the women that I journey with. I live in Vancouver and have been employed with UBC since 2008, working on various community based research projects. I am one of the founding members of Women in2 Healing working in the community to assist women offenders to end the stigmatization of incarcerated women.

Lara-Lisa Condello

I am an Instructor and the Justice Studies Department Head at Nicola Valley Institute of Technology (NVIT)—BC's Aboriginal post-secondary institute. I founded NVIT's prison education program. I participate on prison program advisory committees and am a co-investigator on a participatory action research team at UBC. Advocating prison human rights, I am concerned with issues such as health. A practitioner of Indigenous collaborative learning, I apply artistic media to address the provocative yet often misunderstood concepts of penal abolition and transformative justice. I am passionate about progressive social change and am committed to promoting life-long learning and grassroots community development.

Linnea Groom

As a mother of two adult sons, wife, and sister of two brothers, I felt challenged at the thought of relating exclusively to females, when asked to coordinate the W2 volunteer program in a women's institution. My two-decade involvement with people in incarceration began on a volunteer basis, along with my husband. My passion for relating to people who are marginalized in this way came from my lived experience of being a visual racial minority in the community where I spent much of my childhood. I find joy in affirming women in their value and abilities.

Lisa Torikka

I have been a resident at the Gateway of Hope as part of the Opportunities Program since my release from ACCW. Since that time, I have worked hard. I completed (with honours) a twenty-week Cooks Training Program, I have become a first year apprentice with ITA as a cook, I work part-time jobs, and have full-time employment starting in September with Kwantlen University, and achieved many smaller goals such as getting ID, learning how to budget, obtaining a driver's license etc. I now know how valuable supported living is. I always thought, in the past, that I could do it on my own, I know differently now. This has been one of the biggest changes I made in my life, to let others help me, to humble myself, and allow people to guide me. I have many more goals to accomplish and believe that one of them is helping women that come out of prison. I don't really know what that looks like yet, but I do know that by just doing what I am doing, by living my life the way it was meant to be lived is helping to inspire other women to try and do the same, and for now, that is enough.

Marie Fayant (Holy Cow)

I am a Cree descendent from Saskatoon Saskatchewan. I have two beautiful sons, six grandchildren, and one great-grandchild born. I have worked with our Métis Society in Surrey, the community with Kla-how-eya with the children and families, I worked for a short time as a Counsellor at Native Education Centre, and I take part in Ceremonies whenever requested at Langara College and Simon Fraser University. I am involved with the First Nations Breast Cancer Society as a Director. I started to work in the women's correctional centre when two wonderful co-workers, and one woman in prison who had cancer, convinced me that they needed an Elder/Spiritual Advisor. I have worked in provincial and federal centres and volunteered for many years in the male correctional institutions. I invite inmates to come to sweats in the community with their families when they are released from prison.

Marnie Scow

I am twenty-four years old, and I have been out of prison and living clean off drugs and alcohol for almost three years. I attend Douglas College; I am completing my BA in Criminology, with a minor in Psychology, before attending law school at University of British Columbia. I hope to become a criminal defense attorney. I am actively involved in both my community and school as well as with Women in2 Healing. I have shared my story and my experience, strength, and hope with several organizations across the province in hopes of helping others realize that there is another way to live. I am also employed fulltime as an assistant manager in a Greek tavern.

Melissa Glover

Melissa was a strong woman with a beautiful smile who was passionate about life. Melissa loved making everyone laugh with "tearful, non-stop giggles." Melissa's poetry reflects much of her journey through life: "the good, bad and the ugly." Melissa was an enthusiastic member of the participatory research team, and her passion was to become healthy so that she could spend more time with her daughter. Melissa's life ended tragically and too early. She is missed by many.

Rene Chan

I am a gentle and loving woman and help others whenever I can. I trained as an inmate peer educator and believe that education is a way for incarcerated women to improve their lives and their own health. I have been through hell and back, only making me more compassionate and less judgemental. Although we hear "no you can't, you'll never make it..." we have proven that we can! Everybody's dreams are possible and I am living well into my dreams today.

Annette Dubrule

After I was released from prison, I worked for two years as a research assistant on the Doing Time participatory research project in Prince George, BC, and then I worked as a receptionist for a law firm for eighteen months. I am hoping to take the Medical Laboratory Assistant program online through Thompson Rivers University, and have arranged a practicum for this in Quesnel, BC. I spend as much time as I can with my son, who stays with me every alternate week, and I communicate daily with my daughter who lives in Ontario with her father. I stay in shape, when not working or taking courses, by attending the gym regularly, climbing Cut Banks, and going for long walks and hikes. I have always had an interest for photography and I enjoy taking and then modifying pictures. I still live with my mom out in Blackburn, where we own a log home that requires much maintenance, which I enjoy doing. I recently applied for a pardon.

Terry Howard

I began prison outreach as a volunteer twelve years ago and jumped at the opportunity to coordinate the prison outreach program for the Positive Living Society of BC. I started working with the women at Alouette Correctional Centre for Women in 2005 and was immediately captivated by the organic information dissemination among the women who were part of the community-based research project Women in2 Healing. I was stunned at the new passion to pass on the information from their presentations to the other women incarcerated with them in an informal, yet incredibly effective educational blitz. In my years of prison outreach, I had never seen an uptake of information as effective as what happened among the women with their newfound knowledge of the power of education. They were passionate, informed and intent on letting other women know of the dangers inherent in their own issue. This experience forever transformed my approach to working with people in prison. I am now the Director of Community-Based Research for Positive Living BC (formerly BC Persons With AIDS Society).

Vivian Ramsden

I am a Registered Nurse and received a Ph.D. in Interdisciplinary Studies from the University of Saskatchewan. I am a Professor and Director of the Research Division, Department of Academic Family Medicine at the University of Saskatchewan. My background spans both critical care in acute care settings and primary health care in urban, rural, First Nations, and international communities. My research interests are:

primary health care, participatory processes of research and evaluation; mixed methods; and, prevention of chronic diseases. I spend a portion of each year working at Omayal Achi College of Nursing in Chennai, India.

Tanya Newell

I had been in and out of jail since I was a juvenile in 2005. When I had Mason at the age of thirty, I had already served over ten years in institutions: I was institutionalized and I was completely oblivious to the fact that things needed to change. My plan on my release day was always to get high, to return to place of my offence and arrest (where my "friends" were) and to continue the cycle of addiction and crime that I knew. The chance to bring my baby back to the prison after his birth changed my life for the better. Having Mason with me at ACCW allowed for bonding that we otherwise wouldn't have had an opportunity to have. Had I not been allowed to go to the prison with my infant son, the bonding would not have been there: my plans would have completely changed for release and I would probably still be in the (correctional) system today. Having Mason with me in prison, made me be more accountable in my release planning and I had to orchestrate a plan that was suitable for both him and I. It made me really have to look at the options, read the literature and look into what these houses had to offer—I was responsible for another life. From ACCW, we went to Peardonville Treatment facility, because they accept babies there at three months old. I have been out of jail since then, with the exception of one return for charges that I'd already had prior to Mason's birth. I am drug and alcohol free. I am happy and healthy. I have my children in my life: Mitch, Mason, and now Tyson. Mason is a wonderful little boy; he is caring and kind, good-natured and well behaved: a happy normal little boy that was not negatively affected by the circumstance.